FAR SCAPE™

THE ILLUSTRATED SEASON 4 COMPANION

FARSCAPE: THE ILLUSTRATED SEASON 4 COMPANION

1 84023 591 8
1 84023 698 1 (Diamond edition)

Published by
Titan Books
A division of
Titan Publishing Group Ltd
144 Southwark St
London
SE1 0UP

First edition May 2003
2 4 8 10 9 7 5 3 1

Photographs supplied by The Jim Henson Company and *Farscape* Productions.

ACKNOWLEDGEMENTS

None of these books would have been possible without the time and co-operation of the *Farscape* cast and crew, which has continued since the series' cancellation. Special thanks to those who helped track everyone down for this book: Annabel Davis, Dave Elsey, David Franklin, Tracy Gilbert, Deb Peart, Andrew Prowse and Emanda Thomas. Thanks also to: Omar Camacho at Henson's LA for sorting out the tapes, and Dan Bateman and Matthew Basham at Henson's London. Monica Gillen and the Creation team for their help at all the *Farscape* conventions, and this year to Kerry Glover and Jill Sherwin for making sure I got there! Lee Binding, Martin Eden, Rod Edgar, Mark Juddery and Chip Schneider for multi-media assistance, Arne Ratermanis and the Save *Farscape* Media Relations Team for the Wanted posters and Jerry Boyajian, Jenn Fletcher, and especially Katrina Gerhard for the Anglo-American Alliance. The book wouldn't exist without sterling help from Helen Grimmett, and as ever my thanks to Adam Newell, David Barraclough, Jo Boylett and Oz Browne at Titan. But most of all thanks to Rockne S. O'Bannon, Ben Browder and David Kemper for being available for questions and discussion despite all the many other new calls on their time.

DEDICATION

For Ali. My Aeryn.

Did you enjoy this book? We love to hear from our readers. Please e-mail us at: **readerfeedback@titanemail.com** or write to Reader Feedback at the above address. To subscribe to our regular newsletter for up-to-the-minute news, great offers and competitions, email: **titan-news@titanemail.com**

Titan Books' film and TV range are available from all good bookshops or direct from our mail order service. For a free catalogue or to order, phone **01536 764646** with your credit card details, or write to **Titan Books Mail Order, AASM Ltd, Unit 6, Pipewell Industrial Estate, Desborough, Northants, NN14 2SW**. Please quote reference FS/C4

A CIP catalogue record for this title is available from the British Library.

Printed and bound in Great Britain by MPG, Bodmin, Cornwall.

FARSCAPE™

THE ILLUSTRATED SEASON 4 COMPANION

Paul Simpson

Series created by Rockne S. O'Bannon

TITAN BOOKS

CONTENTS

ugust 1998, Sydney, Australia. A wet, windy, nasty winter day (remember, this is Australia). I find myself riding shotgun in a cheap, tinny rental car which is winding its way through industrial back streets of Sydney. Beside me, Tom Brown, first art director for the "soon to be series" *Farscape*, is driving and telling stories of his life back in England. This is what you do in show business, you meet people and you get to know them as quickly as you can, because in days you will have gone your separate ways, to the opposite ends of the globe. 'Carpe diem' and all that yotz... 'cause before you know it, you're saying 'goodbye'. But this rainy day is ' hello'. Tom is taking me for my first look at Moya.

As we turn onto a street lined with massive live oaks near the warehouse complex in which the Moya sets are being constructed, the random nature of the universe reveals itself. A massive tree branch crashes into the road directly in front of us. Tom slams on the brakes, and the crappy rental car comes screeching to a halt, the nose of our vehicle fully buried in dense foliage. The road is completely blocked, sidewalk to sidewalk, by several tons of immovable live oak. We were, in actual terms, split seconds from being crushed, maimed and/or disfigured. For Tom and me at least, *Farscape* almost never happened.

A few minutes later, having bonded in true film-maker (we almost died) fashion and having navigated a longer route to the construction facilities, Tom ushered me into a warehouse, where I was placed under the raw, unpainted ribs of what was to become Moya's Command. She seemed massive. Her shape was unlike any I had ever stood in before or since. Perhaps it was my near brush with dismemberment by oak tree. Perhaps it was being so far removed from any place familiar to me. But standing under Moya's bones for the first time, I felt both safe and jittery... Amazing things could happen here.

What followed was the most astonishing four years of my life. Eighty-eight episodes of *Farscape* were produced. Every one of them difficult. Every one of them a-teetering on the edge of glorious failure. *Farscape* was a labour of passion. It had to be, because shooting *Farscape* was hell and Hell is a very hot place I hear, something akin to Homebush in the summertime. The making of *Farscape* was a logistical nightmare. The hours were intense and long. The working conditions could be harsh and unpleasant. The shooting schedule was most often out of date by the time it was peeled off the Xerox machine. Change was a constant and flexibility a requirement. Chaos was our constant companion. I had never before seen, nor expect to see again, such a television shoot.

Out of the cauldron of production came two very significant things: the world got eighty-eight hours of very witchy television and I got mates. Friendships occur in television production the world over. But I only know of one good place to find mates. Australia imparted to me a deep appreciation

of the term 'mate'. And make no mistake, Australians take their mateship very seriously... So much so, there have been attempts to write it into the Australian Constitution. On *Farscape*, I didn't have colleagues, or collaborators, or co-workers, or buddies, or pals, or friends... I had mates. And me and my mates worked on some wicked sci-fi telly.

September 2002, Homebush Bay, Australia. The sun is shining hard as summer makes an early arrival, and the notorious heat of Homebush is reminding me that I would be soaking with sweat if I were wearing leathers. I drive alone in my cheap, tinny rental car and pull up outside the converted warehouses that have been home to Moya and the crew of *Farscape* for the last few years. Peering into the stages I watch the construction crew rip apart the walls of the sets and toss them into waiting dumpsters. *Farscape* has been cancelled, and Moya is being eaten like road-kill on hot pavement.

Every panel ripped from her ribs has a story. There Crichton slammed Chiana against a bulkhead^{TM}. Over there, D'Argo slammed Sparky against a bulkhead^{TM}. Here Zhaan slammed Crichton against a bulkhead^{TM}. And there, Crichton and Aeryn slammed together into a bulkhead^{TM}. Bulkhead slamming is a *Farscape* trademark. No part of Moya was left unexplored by the cast and the cameras. No piece of floor, no panel, no light fixture, no rib, no piece of her lacks for a multitude of different tales. Cast and crew had crawled above, behind, and beneath her parts, which are now headed for a landfill. We knew her well and lived far longer in her than any could have imagined when the journey began. It cuts deeply to see her go.

January 2003, Los Angeles. I can only imagine that the stages which belonged to Moya and her crew are now empty, or have returned to their previous life housing rice cakes in transit from Indonesia. The walls are no longer black, and light is freely allowed into the cavernous rooms. The construction of alien vessels is a fading memory and assistant directors no longer call the crew to silence. But on a screen somewhere, for some time to come, Moya's story will shine out into a room of strangers, perhaps, to amaze someone for the first time...

In the film business you expect to say goodbye sooner rather than later. Sooner is easier.

Ben Browder
Los Angeles
January 2003

Rockne S. O'Bannon

"What's interesting about season four is that the episodes which came closest to the series' original sense of awe and wonder of a human lost in space were the stories where John Crichton returned to Earth."

EXT. SPACE

The WORMHOLE CLOSES AGAIN, SWALLOWING MOYA COMPLETELY in an instant. Gone. No trace of wormhole or Moya!

CRICHTON
You have got to be kidding me.

And as CRICHTON REACTS to the unthinkable, we FREEZE FRAME, SUPERING *"TO BE CONTINUED"*...

THE END OF SEASON THREE

fter production finished on the third season, *Farscape*'s executive producer David Kemper began working with SCI FI, outlining the ideas he had for the fourth year, and possible later seasons of the show. His efforts were rewarded when the channel ordered two further seasons on 1 October 2001. Although they expressed great confidence in the series' future, they also put a 'kill option' into the agreement, just in case...

Kemper became involved in protracted discussions with SCI FI about exactly what it was that they had ordered. "Their new promotional people didn't seem to understand the show," Kemper notes. "They were worried that new people couldn't get into the show because it was semi-serialised. They wanted us to make it more like *Stargate*."

The channel had recently taken on production of *Stargate SG-1*, and it was their intention to pair the fourth season of *Farscape* with their new series. Kemper was aware that the two shows were very different, although the promotional people had a problem understanding this. "'He's a man who has to save the universe!' was the tagline they suggested," Kemper recalls. "We pointed out that it was nothing to do with the universe: John Crichton just wants to find his girl. Then we got promos that said he slept with any alien babe that came his way. We couldn't understand how they could get that from what we were doing."

Kemper also had to deal with a request that Claudia Black had made during the filming of 'Dog with Two Bones'. She needed to take some time away from filming, and asked if it was possible for Aeryn to come back later in the season. Ever willing to help the show's stars, Kemper looked for a way to make this work.

"I decided I would use this opportunity," he says. "We were going to bring in a new person anyway, just because we like to keep the show fresh. New people keep the show from stagnating. I told the network I would start the first episode with Crichton with a beard, meeting Raelee Hill's character. Anyone new who tuned in would essentially be seeing what could be the pilot for a brand new series. Crichton would not be encumbered with the Aeryn relationship. It would be boy meets girl for the first time, there are some sparks, and we watch them go!"

Kemper was in America dealing with this, and bringing together a new core team of

Above: Crichton meets Sikozu Svala Shanti Sugaysi Shanu.

writers for the year. However in season four, series creator Rockne S. O'Bannon took a significant step back, working on other projects and letting others run with the ball on *Farscape*. "It's always the case with something that's 'your baby'; once you've handed it over to someone else, there are bound to be things done that you don't completely agree with," O'Bannon comments. "But season four certainly maintained *Farscape*'s reputation for never being conventional, and I appreciated that."

Pre-production was proceeding at Homebush Bay ready for filming to begin early in 2002. Season three's producer Tony Winley had left to work on feature films, so Sue Milliken, who had been in charge of the second year, returned to produce alongside Andrew Prowse. Most of the other key personnel returned, with Dave Elsey and the Creature Shop team working on aliens and props, and Tim Ferrier busily designing sets. Ben Browder stopped shaving, so that Crichton's hirsute look could be genuine.

The show's directors and post-production crew were delighted by the switch from full frame filming to widescreen, giving the show a more cinematic quality. The titles for the season were recut, and a new voiceover subtly changed the emphasis of John Crichton's worries. There was an air of rejuvenation about the series, which boded well for the coming year... ∎

THE EPISODES

" It's just fate, as usual, keeping its bargain, but screwing us in the fine print."

– John Crichton

Regular cast: Ben Browder (John Crichton), Claudia Black (Aeryn Sun), Anthony Simcoe (Ka D'Argo), Gigi Edgley (Chiana), Wayne Pygram (Scorpius), Melissa Jaffer (Noranti), Raelee Hill (Sikozu), Jonathan Hardy (Rygel: voice), Lani Tupu (Pilot: voice)

Written by: David Kemper	**Guest cast:** Peter Whittle (Ilkog), Bob Nisevic (Nukana),
Directed by: Andrew Prowse	Dinah Shearing (voice of Elack's Pilot)

ome time after Moya disappeared, John Crichton is heading back in his module to his new home, the dying Leviathan Elack, whose aged Pilot warns him that they do not have much time remaining. Crichton believes he has nearly cracked "Wormholes for Dummies", and is busily writing out the equations in Elack's maintenance bay, assisted by a DRD he has nicknamed 1812. Crichton's work is disturbed by the sudden arrival of a ship through the Leviathan's walls, bringing on board Sikozu Svala Shanti Sugaysi Shanu. She is amazed to find anyone on board the Leviathan, and tries to persuade Crichton to hide from the people following her, who will not hesitate to kill him. The Grudeks want to strip the Leviathan of its toubray tissue, but Crichton is determined his new home will not be violated in this way. He and Sikozu try to stay one step ahead of the Grudeks, but their hiding place is revealed when Chiana's voice suddenly come across the comms...

Sikozu to Crichton

"If you are sober or sane enough to understand, I suggest you aim that behind you. The creatures following me execute on sight. Now... what are you going to do for me?"

"I thought Crichton being out there on his own for a long time was a good idea," Ben Browder recalls. "It gave all of our people a chance to develop. There was a mandate to reintroduce the series with season four. With the number of characters in *Farscape*, we had to give the new audience a chance to catch up. I think that's one of the reasons we started with Crichton alone and reintroduced the cast one by one."

Both David Kemper and Andrew Prowse describe Browder's performance at the start of the episode as some of the best work that the actor had ever done on *Farscape*, and certainly Browder was given plenty of material to

ENCOUNTERS: BRINDZ HOUND

A blood-tracking beast used by the Leviathan-hunting Grudeks to clean out inhabited Leviathans. The Brindz Hound springs off walls, propelling itself forward in a state of continuous motion, only stopping when it makes its kill.

work with, starting with his manic conducting of the red, white and blue painted DRD, 1812.

"Before I wrote 'Crichton Kicks', I went and bought six different versions of the 1812 Overture," writer and executive producer David Kemper explains, "and I listened to it five to ten times a day for two months! I wanted the script to have the rhythms of the 1812 Overture. I let Tchaikovsky's music infuse itself into me."

The piece turns up throughout the episode. "I thought we'd need at least seven or eight instances of the 1812, but in fact I think there's only three playings," composer Guy Gross notes, "but even with only those three times, you get the sense this DRD has been learning how to play it. By the final time, it's practically as orchestral as Crichton has in his head."

At one point, Crichton yells at the Grudeks to get off the Leviathan — in Klingon! "That wasn't scripted," Browder explains. "I saw these guys and I thought they were Klingons! I got on the phone to Ricky Manning and said 'I've got to have some Klingon'. He e-mailed me back with sound files and a pronunciation guide. I told Andrew Prowse, but I don't think I told Raelee I was going to do it. Her reaction is pretty damn honest. Poor girl — she shows up and all of a sudden I'm screaming in Klingon!"

Above: Crichton and Sikozu in hiding from the Grudeks.

Next page: The Grudeks scour Elack's corridors.

Post-production supervisor Deb Peart nominates the episode as one of her favourites of the entire series. "It was well lit, and so well conceived in terms of the set and production design," she notes. "We built several sets on that episode which we thought would be good, because they could be turned into regulation Moya sets," production designer Tim Ferrier explains. "We thought the double-storey set that was like a honeycomb, where the guys were cutting all the meat out of Elack, was now established in this particular physiological part of the Leviathan. If we wanted to, we could have reused it... but I don't think we ever did."

The visual effects team had to spend a great deal of time working on the Brindz Hound, which of course was not there on set for Ben Browder to work with. "The CG guys did a great job putting it in," Browder says. "Can you imagine how I felt on the day doing all that dodging the doggy stuff? It was great. When there's not another actor there I can really go off-*piste*. There's some really embarrassing stuff I tried! The great thing about *Farscape* is that I can put myself in Andrew's hands and know I will not end up looking a complete dork!"

"Soup to nuts, it took a long time to put this together," Kemper concludes. "We were really proud of it." ∎

WHAT WAS LOST PART 1: SACRIFICE

Written by: Justin Monjo	Guest cast: Tammy MacIntosh (Jool), Rebecca Riggs
Directed by: Rowan Woods	(Grayza), David Franklin (Braca), Steve Le Marquand (Oo-Nii), Elizabeth Alexander (Vella), Kim De Lury (Tarnat), Dinah Shearing (voice of Elack's Pilot)

Elack and her Pilot agree to take Crichton to try to find Jool on the planet Arnessk, Moya's last known position, but when they arrive there is no sign of the Leviathan. Sikozu and Rygel remain on board Elack while Crichton and Chiana go down to the surface, where they are joyfully reunited with Jool and D'Argo, who have been studying under Instructor Vella, a renowned archaeologist. The planet was once the homeworld of an order of priests, who by mysterious means maintained peace between Scarrans and Peacekeepers for 500 generations. Their vigil was disrupted, however, when three probes — the 'Darnaz Triangle' — crashed to the surface and created a rhythmic magnetic effect that routinely makes the planet uninhabitable. Vella has found two of the Darnaz probes, but one remains hidden. Crichton seeks out the mysterious old woman who was on board when Moya was swallowed by a wormhole. Escorted by a cowering, amphibious alien, Oo-Nii, the old woman seems determined to prevent Vella from finding the final probe...

> **Crichton to Grayza**
>
> "What do you want from me?"
>
> "What I want may not be as bad as you think. You might even like it."

"We had a tremendous production scheduling difficulty with that two-parter," Ben Browder points out. "We were shooting a lot of exteriors, which is difficult with prosthetics and creature effects, compounded with rain and variable weather. And we were shooting in water, which is never easy — and particularly hard for a guy in a creature suit!"

"I became completely consumed with the almost ridiculous task of creating these worlds," director Rowan Woods comments. "It was almost a per-

ENCOUNTERS: OO-NII

An amphibious creature from the planet Arnessk. At first appearing meek, mild and totally harmless, he is in fact a cold-blooded killer. His race can survive the unrelenting magnetic summers on Arnessk by retreating to the safety of the sea when the magnetics become too high.

verse exercise in raising the bar to the point where we had to fail, but we did it anyway! You use most of your energies making the story work. *Lord of the Rings* took three years to create their world with huge models; on *Farscape* you're asked to do it in three weeks."

In fact the pre-production time on 'What Was Lost' was rather longer than usual, since David Kemper had initially planned to tell the story as the closing episode of season three and the start of season four. At the time, he couldn't make the story work properly, but as the new year began, Justin Monjo offered to write the scripts based on Kemper's file card notes. One major change was the cliffhanger at the end of part one: in the original version, Crichton and Aeryn would have been turned into crystal. This was an idea Kemper kept up his sleeve for later...

The Creature Shop had already begun work on Oo-Nii at the end of the third year. "We'd done hands, feet and a whole body, and it was going to have an animatronic head," fabrication supervisor Lou Elsey recalls. "When we came back to it for the fourth season, the producers wanted it to really fly under water and do loads of action stuff, so we decided it would be better to use a prosthetic make-up, and create a suit which was lot more flexible.

"The suit wasn't made out of foam latex, because that would have just

FARSCAPE FARSCAPE FARSCAPE
FARSCAPE FARSCAPE
FARSCAPE FARSCAPE FARSCAPE
FARSCAPE APP FARSCAPE APE
FARSCAPE FARSCAPE FARSCAPE FARSCAPE
FARSCAPE

held all the water. It was made out of a reticulated foam," she continues. "All the muscles and shapes were carved out of this foam, which was covered in Lycra, artworked and then covered in a Hot Flesh [the Creature Shop's special translucent compound] hybrid coating of rubber over the top, to make it look like it's wet and really shiny. When the actor went into the water, the suit would absorb the water very easily, but when he got out, it would drain out very quickly as well."

One surprising element of the episode was the inclusion of scenes between Scorpius, Grayza and Braca in the 'Previously on *Farscape*' reprise. These had been filmed for 'Crichton Kicks' but hadn't made it into the episode. "We always have things that get dropped, and we just decided we'd use that scene there, because it really clears up stuff in the Peacekeeper world," David Kemper explains. "It was made for a certain place and time, so it wouldn't work as an ordinary flashback."

A lot of the story was filmed on location in Marubra, and Anthony Simcoe enjoyed the opportunity to work away from Homebush. "In season one we did lots of location work, but we hadn't done much the season before," he recalls. "The look we got was spectacular. It was really exciting being out in all weathers on the cliffs and near the beach." ∎

Opposite page: Grayza takes pleasure in seducing Crichton…

Above: …and torturing Scorpius.

WHAT WAS LOST PART II: RESURRECTION

Written by: Justin Monjo **Directed by:** Rowan Woods	**Guest cast:** Tammy MacIntosh (Jool), Rebecca Riggs (Grayza), David Franklin (Braca), Steve Le Marquand (Oo-Nii), Dinah Shearing (voice of Elack's Pilot)

fter surviving his fall from a cliff, Crichton is attacked by the usually obsequious Oo-Nii, who is convinced that he intends to give the probes to Grayza. D'Argo and Sikozu intervene just in time, arriving with a plan to get everyone off the planet. They convince Crichton to keep Grayza occupied, which they know won't be difficult in his current dazed condition. While D'Argo and Rygel put the rest of the plan into operation, Grayza tries to persuade Crichton to help her, offering to find Aeryn for him if he does. Jool realises that time is running out for all of them when she notices that colour is fading from their clothes. The magnetics are rising, and the planet will soon be uninhabitable. Crichton isn't fooled by Grayza, and accuses her of merely being a puppet in Scorpius's master plan. To Crichton's amazement, Braca shoots Scorpius, sending the hybrid tumbling into a grave that Crichton has just dug...

Crichton to Grayza

"I wasn't trying to escape. I thought someone was throwing me off a cliff. I live in a strange universe. Things like that are fairly normal."

"We were in the frame of mind at the beginning of season four to set ourselves the most difficult tasks we could, and give them a shot," says Rowan Woods, recalling the tricky, somewhat waterlogged location shoot. "Kevin Costner's *Waterworld* had tens of millions of dollars spent on preparation before they even rolled the camera. The logistics of water nearly always get you, and bite you in the arse! But we had an incredible time on the rocks at Marubra. We took over a whole peninsula. We only had a couple of days for those sequences on the rocks, and the rest we did in the studio."

Catastrophe nearly struck during filming. "Probably the most exhilarating, exciting moment I've ever had outside on location was when we were shooting the monster fight in the water," Woods adds. "We shot that in a rock pool. It was blowing a gale, the tide was going against us and the whole sea was coming in over the pool. Crichton has jumped off the cliff, and is in the water, swimming to shore. I had all the stunt safety officers in the water around me, along with the camera, all strapped to safety lines. Then this freak wave came over the top of us! Everyone in the pool, including Ben who was in his heavy boots, hung onto the lines but disap-

peared from view for about eight seconds as this wall of water washed right over the top of our heads. One of the safety officers got washed up onto the rocks. It was amazing nobody got seriously hurt!"

Above: Grayza and Braca lead Scorpius to his execution.

Ben Browder found the scenes where Crichton is forced by Grayza's potent sweat into having sex with her difficult in a different way. "Crichton is being raped," he points out. "That's a very uncomfortable thing to do on series television. It'd be uncomfortable to do in a film. How do you answer to this kind of material? We were doing it, but I don't think anybody in the end was really happy with it. In true *Farscape* fashion, we went ahead and did it. As an actor, you are there to service the story but I was never comfortable. I think it made Grayza reprehensible."

Next page: Sikozu keeps out of sight in the Arnessk tunnels.

Rowan Woods notes "the second episode was an action romp. If it didn't have that serious B story where Crichton was being put upon in a sexual way by Grayza, it wouldn't have worked. The second and third acts were insane action beats. Fortunately in the first and second acts you had the chance to cut away to the Crichton/Grayza story, which brought the

episode down to earth, and gave you some serious, unsettling stuff. I'm really glad that story was taken as seriously by Ben and Rebecca as it was. They created a very tense, unnerving experience for the viewer."

The episode needed extensive work in post-production to counterbalance the varied weather conditions on location. "One day there'd be beautiful blue sky, then the next day it was overcast," Deb Peart says. "The effects company Frame, Set and Match did about fifty sky replacements in about eight hours to deal with that."

The memorable visual effects of the magnetics were originally going to be created 'in camera' during filming, but the team decided it was easier to handle this in post-production. "Rowan wanted this degradation to come over in about twenty stages, but it was too complicated to work everything on that sort of gradient," Peart adds. "What we ended up doing, after talking to Rowan and the director of photography, Russell Bacon, was to bring it down to about four stages, desaturating the colour, taking the tones out, then bringing it in in abundance."

"This was a huge story," David Kemper concludes. "I joked that it could have been a four-parter!" ■

LAVA'S A MANY SPLENDORED THING

Written by: Michael Miller **Directed by:** Michael Pattinson	**Guest cast:** John Adam (Raa'Keel), Jack Finsterer (Gleeg), Alan Flower (Frool), Ross Newton (Sloggard), Teo Gebert (Weldon), Mick Roughan (Airek)

'Argo lands on a barren, rocky planet so the crew can be sick after trying one of Noranti's concoctions. Rygel stumbles into a nearby cave, where he finds crates filled with treasure. Crichton, D'Argo and Noranti follow in time to see Rygel engulfed by a trap that leaves the Hynerian covered in an unbreakable amber-like substance. Simultaneously, the cave entrance seals up, leaving Chiana and Sikozu on the surface. Noranti identifies markings on the crates, and believes Rygel's captors are Tarkan Freedom Fighters, "good people" who will listen to reason. However two of the Tarkans arrive and open fire on the crew. They have a shielding device and Crichton, D'Argo and Noranti beat a retreat, leaving Rygel to be taken into the depths of the cave. The Dominar meets the brutish Tarkan leader, Raa'Keel, who will stop at nothing — including sacrificing his own men — to kill Crichton and D'Argo...

> **Crichton to D'Argo**
>
> "Ah, more bad news."
>
> "Same dren, different planet."
>
> "Yeah, we're trapped. Again."

'Lava Is a Four-Letter Word' was one of the alternative titles suggested for this episode, and probably best sums up the feelings of most of the people working on it. "'Lava' was an extremely big push for us," production designer Tim Ferrier recalls. "In fact, I think it was the hardest episode I ever did on the show."

"The concept was great," David Kemper notes. "I was always positive it would be a winning episode. But it had so many problems in terms of the logistics of how we were going to pull it off. It gave Tim and the director fits. How do you shoot lava? We had meetings about camera filters and shot tests. Everyone was tense and nervous because the director didn't have a plan — not that he should, but he was new and it was a tough episode for him."

Puppeteer Mat McCoy explains the problem. "Over the years, a methodology had evolved between departments. The same people had been doing the same jobs for so long, and everyone was really excellent at what they did. As a newcomer, you haven't had that chance to build up

a rapport with the cast and crew over a period of time. Plus, it's a big shock to the system to be thrown into sci-fi, which is the most complicated genre you can direct in!"

"Our characters had to get into the lava, have interplay with the lava, throw it at each other, and be killed by it," Ferrier says. "No one could cite an example, even on a big-budget feature film, where these things had been done. The script also demanded a very big labyrinth of caves, and that's a time-consuming project to build! We knew we couldn't go on location — there had to be lava flowing through it, and explosions. I was pleased with the sets though. They looked pretty good in the end."

David Kemper describes 'Lava' as a 'Butch and Sundance' episode. "It's a great buddy story for Crichton and D'Argo: they're solving problems all the way through," Anthony Simcoe confirms. "They're also dealing with the complexities of having Noranti around, as she's a bit of a nightmare for them at that stage. There are some great comical moments Ben and I conjured up for that episode."

"It was a very frustrating one to shoot," Browder adds, recalling some of the cross words on the set. "It's what happens when you don't agree about what the script requires. But Anth and I got a chance to play together.

I like the repartee between Crichton and D'Argo: we could do some of the comedic banter which we didn't really have much opportunity to do later."

Melissa Jaffer enjoyed Noranti's bellydancing routine. "I've been a dancer all my life and I knew the potential there," she recalls. "The thing about *Farscape* that I love is how it shows us that science fiction is *fun*. People might wonder how this old woman can dance. But, as David Kemper kept reminding me, she thinks she's eighteen years of age, and a model on a catwalk!" For the finale of Noranti's dance, the Creature Shop even provided a wild bush of hair for her armpits, but in the end, all we see is Crichton and D'Argo's horrified reaction.

Gigi Edgley had a similarly gross encounter. "The sampling of D'Argo's vomit was a fun moment," she smiles. "I just let Chi take over in that one, much to everyone's disgust in front of and behind camera. It took a quite a few takes to shoot that scene, so I was almost full by lunch!"

"It felt almost like a very quirky retro *Lost in Space* meets *Star Trek* meets *Red Dwarf*," Ben Browder jokes, trying to summarise how the episode turned out. David Kemper concludes, "We did have a lot of trouble shooting it, but in the end, the episode is a gangbuster!" ■

Opposite page: Gleeg fires at the amber encasing Rygel.

Above: D'Argo and Crichton try to negotiate with Raa'Keel.

PROMISES

Written by: Ricky Manning
Directed by: Geoff Bennett

Guest cast: Rebecca Riggs (Grayza), David Franklin (Braca), Richard Carter (Ullom), Anja Coleby (Ponara), Damian Hunter (Rinlo)

rriving back on Moya, Crichton's excitement at seeing Aeryn is instantly soured when Scorpius appears at her side. Aeryn is in the throes of an artificially induced Heat Delirium, and she claims Scorpius saved her life by fitting her with a coolant suit. She makes Crichton promise not to harm him, saying he has come aboard the ship seeking asylum. Scorpius is escorted to one of the Leviathan's cells, where he is regarded with suspicion by everyone except Sikozu. Before the crew can set off on their travels, a giant Lukythian ship rockets into a holding pattern near Moya, its mass preventing StarBurst. Its captain, Ullom, claims Aeryn was recently part of a team of assassins who liquidated the Prime Lukythian. The assassins were infected with an artificial Heat Delirium, but in exchange for the names of those who ordered the hit, he will provide the antidote to Aeryn's life-threatening condition...

Crichton to Scorpius

" Kryptonite? Silver bullet? Buffy? What's it gonna take to keep you in the grave? "

"Geoff Bennett is twisted, sick and dark," David Kemper says of this episode's new-to-*Farscape* director, "and that's the highest praise I can give someone on this show! He is magnificent, and was 'one of us' from the first day."

Bennett's introduction to the series was the episode that finally reunited the crew on board Moya. "The main feature of this story was bringing back Claudia and Wayne to the cast, so that our ship was together again. Then we could really start telling stories," Kemper explains. "This year was like a train pulling out of the station, chugging along, letting everyone get on board and then we could pick up speed." "In some ways, the arc for the season starts in this episode," Ben Browder agrees, "when Aeryn says, 'Promise me you won't hurt him.'"

At the start of the season, the producers had to decide what they were going to do with Scorpius. "We'd destroyed his Command Carrier, so he

ENCOUNTERS: LUKYTHIANS

Ugly aliens with extremely wide-set eyes and mechanical sections implanted directly into their face and skull. Known for their horrendous treatment of other species, including a legendary massacre in the Trola System.

wasn't going to get a promotion with the Peacekeepers," Ricky Manning explains. "He's *persona non grata* with the Peacekeepers at the end of season three. We could easily have killed him off — he could have died in the destruction of the Command Carrier, but we thought he had a couple more miles in him. On *Farscape* characters evolve and do what you might think in advance is the last thing you'd expect, but which in context makes sense. Scorpius is not going to walk away and let events take their course. He's a player — he's going to get involved. The most direct way to do that is to go to Crichton and say, 'I realise I'm not going to be able to coerce anything out of you. I've tried that and failed. All I can do now is keep you safe from enemy forces and hope that when the Scarran bloodbath inevitably begins, you see reason and give my side some help.' That was a pretty gutsy thing for us to do, but we felt Scorpius could justify it."

Manning notes that there are loose ends regarding Scorpius's arrival, and Aeryn's involvement with him before we see them at the start of the episode. "We didn't really explain how Scorpy got involved and saved her," he concedes. "He says he saved her, she backs him up, and that's where we left it. How did the mechanics of it work? Well, we honestly did not design these things so as to leave out a couple of ingredients to drive

Above: Crichton and Aeryn prepare to abandon the Lukythian ship.

Next page: Ullom tries to take his revenge on Aeryn.

the fans mad, so they could debate it endlessly. But if that's how it turns out, we don't mind that either!"

Ricky Manning also wanted to give a fresh twist to the idea of the Crichton/Scorpius hybrid seen in 'Die Me Dichotomy' and 'Infinite Possibilities', and wrote scenes for Aeryn as Scorpius. "I had to get another life cast done for that, and I was determined to try to enjoy it this time," Claudia Black recalls. "Dave Elsey commented that I was one of the first people he'd ever seen to have a smile on their face in the life cast when it came out. I'd had a few episodes off and I came into work very relaxed and happy!"

After the difficulties of 'Lava', Tim Ferrier enjoyed creating the Lukythians' world. "I started off with some ideas about the spaceship and their people being like a squid underwater," he notes, "and that evolved into the designs they did for the computer-generated imagery. We gave the interiors a soft feel. I was trying to get away from what we had done for the past four episodes, which was really earthy, with oaky tones, browns and oranges. I wanted to do something that was cool, blue and aquatic."

"I always wanted to try out Geoff on *Farscape* because I thought he'd really enjoy it," Andrew Prowse concludes. "It blew his mind!" ∎

Written by: Sophie C. Hopkins Directed by: Ian Watson	Guest cast: No guest stars

richton's wormhole research takes a leap forward when he correctly predicts the appearance of a wormhole near Moya. But before he can celebrate, the Leviathan is ensnared by a giant space plant that shorts out systems and starts eating through Moya's skin. As Rygel doesn't seem able to cope with the first crisis of his captaincy, D'Argo insists they try things his way, and goes outside to blast the plant off Moya's hull with Lo'La's cannon. Noranti uses her unorthodox 'herbological' methods to study the plant, revealing an error in D'Argo's tactics. Sikozu's desperate warning arrives too late — D'Argo's ship fires upon the plant, sending it inside Moya and crippling her even further. As Aeryn and Chiana try to plug the leaks inside the hull, Aeryn swears the young Nebari to secrecy before confiding to her that she is pregnant — and that she is not sure whether John Crichton is the father or not...

Sikozu to Crichton

"Do you know what you did wrong?"

"You mean other than getting up this morning?"

"In science fiction, everything often comes down to base human behaviour," composer Guy Gross notes. "At the end of the day, this episode is about gossiping and trust — who places the right trust in whom? They all trust each other and regret it the next morning." It adds an extra dimension to what Ben Browder describes as "a classic ship show."

David Kemper is delighted to note that "Sophie actually came up with this story on her own. She had a lot of enthusiasm. She got our sense of humour, and just how sick our people are! A lot of times with new writers, we are in the room with everyone talking, and we end up helping them to come up with a story. But Sophie wanted to do a story with plants, echoing something with Zhaan. It was a really good concept. We decided to make this like the classic monster movies where you didn't see the adversary that much, and it was stalking you. It was reminiscent of some of the old *Star Trek* episodes — but of course we were going to give it the *Farscape* twist treatment!"

One of those twists came in the sequence where D'Argo enthusiastically sets about destroying the plant with Lo'La's cannon (which had been used to such devastating effect earlier in the year). Guy Gross recalls the tone of his music added to the false expectations in the scene. "We let the audience believe that he's doing the right thing, and it's all going to be fixed, only to discover he's made it worse," he says. "The music helped to lead the audience down the garden path!"

For director Ian Watson, returning for his fourteenth episode, the emotional core of the story was the repercussions of Aeryn's pregnancy. "It's all about Aeryn's emotional journey," he comments. "She knows she's pregnant, and has to deal with it. She doesn't want to talk about it, but has to. She and Crichton have to come to some sort of understanding about it."

Watson praises Browder's and Black's performances in the critical tag scene at the end of the episode. "It's the parting of the ways between those two and it's a wonderful moment," he says. "Ben and Claudia always do that stuff well. We're always rushing, and don't have time to do a lot of coverage with the camera, but they always make it work."

"The tag scene is *very* important," Black notes. "That's the first time we see Aeryn really yielding to Crichton, and ask what she has to do. He leaves it with her, firmly. She's got to get her story straight and get back to him."

The director worked closely with Black and Gigi Edgley on the earlier scenes where Aeryn takes Chiana into her confidence. Edgley notes that "these are the kinds of scenes that disagree with all I have learnt from

my journey through life, so it was difficult for me taking the jump. I don't think Chi knows what to do with the secret! But when she realises how she has betrayed her friend, she has no idea how to take her words back."

The Chinese whispers sequence was a late addition to the script, which went through many different permutations before shooting began. "This probably gave us the most fits of any story of the year," David Kemper says. "There were so many scenes and so many strands to weave together, but in the end we got it right. We went down a lot of roads, because there were so many options. Every time we came up with one way to tell the story, we'd think of another one which might be better."

Visually, 'Natural Election' is one of the darkest stories the series has ever told. "There are bits where you can't see anything at all, which is pretty extraordinary in *Farscape*," Andrew Prowse comments. "I remember [director of photography] Russell Bacon asking if I'd seen the rushes, and whether I thought it was too dark. I said it was fine, but when I looked at a few bits later, I thought, 'Oh my God, there's almost nothing there!' But it works for that story, because it needed atmosphere above everything else." ■

Opposite page: Aeryn examines Pilot's injuries.

Above: *Crichton and Aeryn survey Moya's infected corridors.*

JOHN QUIXOTE

Written by: Ben Browder	Guest cast: Virginia Hey (Zhaan), Lani Tupu (Crais),
Directed by: Tony Tilse	Tammy MacIntosh (Jool), Paul Goddard (Stark), Rowan
	Woods (Big Zhaan), Alyssa-Jane Cook (Gilina)

While Crichton flies a transport pod back to Moya, Chiana nags him to try out a virtual reality game she has recently acquired. A transmission comes through from D'Argo concerning a problem with Scorpius, but despite this news, Chiana mischievously pulls Crichton into one of the games, against his will. Dressed as medieval knights, Crichton and Chiana appear in a fantastic game world where they are greeted by the game's 'Avatar',

Crichton to Rygel

"I am King Arthur of Camelot. This is my loyal vassal, Patsy."

"Bollocks. You're a pimped out, arrogant fleshie who wants to use my road where none shall pass."

Stark. The Banik lays down the ground rules, explaining the level design is based partly on the memories of the John Crichton who died saving DamBaDa. Finding himself unable to leave the game world due to a glitch, Crichton has no choice but to set off with Chiana, apparently on a quest to either 'Kiss the Princess' or find a green door. In what appears to be a multi-storey car park, they encounter a large male version of Pa'u Zotoh Zhaan, who initially tries to poison Crichton before eventually assisting them. A Rygel-shaped Black Knight then bars the way with fiery farts. Passing him, they find themselves in the lair of the Wicked Witch, who bears a striking resemblance to D'Argo...

(Turn to the 'Script to Screen' section for a detailed look at the making of this episode.) ■

I SHRINK THEREFORE I AM

Written by: Christopher Wheeler **Directed by:** Rowan Woods	**Guest cast:** Duncan Young (Axikor), John Schwarz (Bintog)

Crichton and Noranti are alerted by Pilot to the presence of hostiles on board Moya. Noranti places herself into a coma so she can survive outside the ship, and Crichton then sends his transport pod crashing into a strange attack craft leeched to Moya's hull. Using the diversion to steal back on board, he finds his friends held by armoured bounty hunters, who torture their captives in an attempt to flush him out. Crichton stays in hiding but is found by Scorpius, who forced an exit to his cell and has also been in hiding. With the aid of the DRD 1812, they manage to liquidate one of the intruders, but only then does the enemy play its trump card. They shrink the other crewmembers and place them into holding cells inside their own torsos. The head bounty hunter, Axikor, transmits a warning: "Killing one of us means you'll be killing one or more of your friends"...

Pilot to Crichton

" Ka D'Argo is currently helping Rygel with his laundry, and Aeryn's writing some poetry."

" Uh-huh. What about Chiana and Sikozu?"

" Enjoying each other's company. Preparing a meal for everyone but Rygel. He's not hungry."

"We wanted to do a story where the bad guys weren't idiots," David Kemper recalls. "The initial concept was *Die Hard*. The hook for the audience was that when Crichton arrives, these guys have already subdued Aeryn and D'Argo. They're that good!"

In the early drafts of the script, the whole bodies of the alien bounty hunters opened up, and their captives, still full size, would be put inside. "The problem was that we would only be able to build one mechanical body that could take a person," Kemper notes. "I was looking at the script up on the board in the writers' room and then said, 'What if we did shrinking people?'" The episode immediately changed direction, paying homage to the classic 1960's TV series, *Land of the Giants*. "That was the clever twist,"

ENCOUNTERS: COREESHI BOUNTY HUNTERS

A formidable force, who consist of an organic core surrounded by a bio-engineered armour shell. They have acute hearing and also possess reduction technology. Once reduced, the Coreeshi's prey can be stored and safely transported in containers placed in their chest cavities. The reduction technology is controlled from a panel imbedded into the forearm of their exoskeleton.

director Rowan Woods comments. "It scared the life out of everyone when David suggested it though!"

"We didn't know how it was going to work while we were shooting it," Ben Browder says. "It's a sci-fi cliché, and we don't normally do those on *Farscape*." "I was concerned about that," Woods adds, "and I was concerned about the simplicity of the main story, with Crichton overcoming these battlebots. But it started to come together, and we worked out a simple CGI formula to do the shrinking. We couldn't hang around on the screen too long with those kind of shrinking shots, because it would have looked pretty hokey."

The subplot to the episode, as Crichton and Scorpius reluctantly team up to combat the invaders, was "in a weird way what made it work," Woods considers. "Ben and Wayne created an amusing and diverting little tag team. It became a fun ride — they didn't take it too seriously."

Wayne Pygram felt uncomfortable with the idea of Scorpius having a working gun. "Ben and I said, 'Would it be okay if it didn't have any bullets in it?'" he recalls, "and boom, there was the solution." Browder adds, "I love Wayne's reaction when Crichton gives him the weapon. Giving him a dud weapon wasn't in the script, but I was thinking Crichton had promised Aeryn that *he* wouldn't kill Scorpius. He didn't promise that he wouldn't let someone

else kill him! It was a perfect set up. John could get him killed, but was still keeping his promise."

The battle between Crichton and the Scarran Axikor as they kept switching size was "the most complicated fight sequence we have ever done," Browder comments. "We shot it so quickly, and if Duncan Young hadn't been so capable, able to cope with the prosthetic, act and do all the fights, we never would have got it finished."

"If you aren't used to working with Ben, and you've got a chunk of metal over your head and a huge suit, it isn't easy to keep up with him," Claudia Black notes. "Duncan was so dextrous and adaptable. It was an inspiration to see someone dealing with the suit better than any of us could."

One of the most memorable sights from the episode is Aeryn riding on top of a DRD. "That was going to be quite a long sequence," Black remembers, "but I was sick that day, so they modified it." "It was cute," Guy Gross says of the resulting sequence. "I think I got about as silly as I ever got in the music with her call to arms as she hops on top of the DRD."

"I'm Pollyanna," David Kemper jokes. "Everyone said this would stink, but I thought it would be the best episode of the year. We took *Land of the Giants* and did it the *Farscape* way!" ∎

Opposite page: The Coreeshi capture Scorpius.

Above: Rygel undergoes interrogation by the bounty hunters.

A PREFECT MURDER

Written by: Mark Saraceni
Directed by: Geoff Bennett

Guest cast: Peter Whitford (Jabuka Clan Chieftain), Bruce Spence (Prefect Falaak), Ivar Kants (Gaashah), Brett Stiller (Zerbat), Jason Chong (E'Alet)

With Moya immobilised in Tormented Space, the crew visit a planet, inhabited by historically warring clans who are now experiencing a fragile peace, hoping to trade for desperately needed supplies. Their arrival coincides with preparations for the election of a new Prefect. Popular clan leader Gaashah looks the likely successor, but faces a strong challenge from the Chieftain of the Jabuka Clan. Chiana manages to upset Gaashah by sleeping with members of his clan indiscriminately, and is banished back to Moya, though she later manages to return to the planet. Aeryn begins experiencing strange hallucinations, then without warning opens fire upon a meeting of the clans. When it is over, Gaashah lies dead, with D'Argo wounded. Aeryn escapes during the confusion, leaving her crewmates under suspicion. The leadership of the clan falls to Gaashah's reluctant son, Zerbat, who must work with Crichton and a local priest, Paroos, to find Aeryn before the Jabuka Clan hunts her down...

D'Argo to Crichton

" I think we should go. "

" What if I don't want to, Cap'n? "

" He respects me. It would help if I could show him I have you under some sort of control, more or less. "

"I like what this episode was, and I like what it could have been," David Kemper comments. "It represents what I like about *Farscape*: it took a risk. When people see an episode they don't like, it's because we took a risk. But equally, if they see an episode they do like, it's because we took a risk."

Mark Saraceni's début script for the series took a very challenging central concept. "Mark had the vision of telling the story in multiple flashback," Kemper says. "It's a great story device, but very hard to do. As time went on, we realised it was going to be tougher than we thought."

"Apparently the intention of those scenes was to expedite matters on set, and make it easier to film because we'd be doubling up on a lot of stuff,"

ENCOUNTERS: E'ALET

A strange alien found on the planet of Prefects, somewhere in Tormented Space. E'Alet has formed a symbiotic relationship with the S'Gabba flies, using their mind-altering capabilities to further the political ambitions of whoever is willing to pay.

Claudia Black recalls. "Unfortunately they were all different, and we couldn't possibly schedule them that way. Ben and I had to lock down our performances, which took out a lot of the tension and creativity."

Going on location with the puppets is always difficult, but the puppeteers enjoyed working with Paroos, the alien priest. "He was based on the character Father Jack from the British comedy show *Father Ted*," Dave Elsey confirms. "David Kemper wanted another creature that flew around on a throne sled, like Rygel."

"We reconstructed the physical operation rig from Rygel," Mat McCoy recalls. "Paroos floated better than Rygel did, and was a wonderful puppet. The animatronics were fantastic — its face could move from grotesque to subtle in a moment."

Gigi Edgley agrees: "I thought the animatronics were *amazing*. I had a great time shooting this episode. I had just done a convention in England, and returned to the set, after spending four days travelling, rather dazed and confused. I allowed the alien to seep through, and I danced with her. The location was great to shoot in, although it was very hot — we constantly collided with challenges with the charcoal trees and the make-up."

'A Prefect Murder' benefited from some of the most stunning location work seen on *Farscape*, as the unit visited an area which had been burned in

Above: The enigmatic alien priest Paroos.

Next page: Prefect Falaak and E'Alet plot their next move.

the bush fires the previous year. "I think that was the most successful exterior forest we did on the series," post-production supervisor Deb Peart says. "It gave the environment those people were living in a rustic, washed out, burned out look."

The post-production crew worked hard to help explain to the audience the nature of the hallucinations. "We put a treatment on all those scenes," Peart notes. "The editor, Wayne Le Clos, made them black and white, which gave a defined distinction between what was real and what was not."

Guy Gross contributed musically. "I liked scoring the melody for the child," he says. "It's there at the opening when Aeryn is by her ship, and then we used it as a way to remind the audience about the flashback nature of the episode. I then returned to it when he returns to his mother." Gross even sang the tune himself. "It's amazing what you can do with software!"

"I always try to make a big effort for a director's first episode," Tim Ferrier explains, "and make sure they get all the facilities, bells and whistles that they possibly can. That didn't quite happen on Geoff Bennett's first episode ['Promises'], so 'A Prefect Murder' was a bit of payback. We made some huge sets: we cut the dome set from 'John Quixote' in half, put a big glass window in it and that became the eyrie of these people!"

"Ultimately it came together," David Kemper concludes. "We had some great performances. But it was a challenging piece of work." ■

Written by: Emily Skopov	Guest cast: Barry Otto (Doctor Tumii), David Field
Directed by: Ian Watson	(Ho'Ock), Chris Mayer (Mekken), Sara Groen (Mujombre),
	Kelly Butler (Selvah), Susan Prior (Kiryah)

Moya desperately needs modifications to stave off madness caused by Tormented Space. The only suitable mechanics within range are on the planet Khurtanan. The crew is quarantined while the local doctor, Tumii, examines them for signs of 'Space Madness'. Scorpius is barred from the planet because of his Scarran ancestry and while the others are waiting, they share a meal of alien molluscs. They almost instantaneously suffer a violent physical reaction. Each crewmember becomes bodily linked to one of the others, Crichton to Sikozu, Aeryn to Rygel and D'Argo to Noranti. Once they are ill, Doctor Tumii reveals he has the only cure to their illness, and if they are not treated quickly they will die. The crew pay up, and Tumii prepares the cure for the molluscs that D'Argo and Noranti ate, but not before D'Argo discovers Noranti has found a new use for a blender...

Rygel to Crichton

"We need to blend in."

"Blend in? Hell, when we got here the clocks stopped. We couldn't blend in on Butt Ugly Night."

"We don't know how life is going to turn out. It's the same with this script. Just go with it," was Ian Watson's advice to his cast on the first day of shooting of this light-hearted episode, which the director describes as "one of my personal favourites."

'Coup by Clam' centred on renowned Australian actor Barry Otto's performance as Doctor Tumii. "He's a wonderful actor, and fulfilled the brief beautifully," Watson says. "He went completely over the top, and created a character that made the episode really work." "Once I saw the costume and I had make-up tests, I went with a certain sort of voice," Otto recalls. "The Dickensian thing was in my subconscious a lot."

The idea of characters swapping emotions had been discussed by Watson and David Kemper some time previously. "He always said that he

ENCOUNTERS: QATAL MOLLUSCS

A shellfish-like food that is perfectly safe as long as both halves are only consumed by one individual. Should the flesh be divided between different stomachs, the food poisoning that results is fatal. Each mollusc harbours a colony of bacteria. When separated, each half's bacteria transmits to the other in an attempt to reunite. The symptoms of Qatal poisoning can be mistaken for Space Madness.

wanted me to direct the episode when we did it," Watson notes. "They came up with the idea of these molluscs, and had some good gags, like Noranti pleasuring herself and people experiencing the same thing on different sides of the planet!" Anthony Simcoe enjoyed the chance to play for laughs once more: "I love doing all that stuff! I'm always looking for opportunities like that, and D'Argo lends himself to some great moments of comedy."

"We wanted to have fun with this episode," David Kemper says. "We knew 'A Prefect Murder' was very dark, and I knew 'Unrealized Reality' needed to be darker and more mysterious because it was going to be the mid-season cliff-hanger. I wanted to slot in a comedy before the end of that first half of the season."

The scenes in the nightclub went through various changes along the way. "I saw that a little differently from the way it ended up being," Kemper notes. "It was meant to be like *Some Like It Hot*." Ben Browder laughs when he recalls the filming of those scenes. "I had to walk from the trailers down the road to the club," he says. "I was fully in drag, with my hair blowing in the wind. The construction workers were whistling at me, and I realised as I walked along that I was being passed by another guy

who looked better than me — which wouldn't have been difficult."

Filming took place in the King's Cross area of Sydney, where the cast didn't look particularly out of place. "When I had some time off, my make-up artist and I went to a café in the street parallel to where we were, and I was sitting wearing my full leathers!" Claudia Black recalls. "It felt like we were jumping over the school fence to play hooky!"

To emphasise the strangeness of the episode, Ian Watson played with the camera angles. "Every shot has a tilt to it," he points out. "If the camera is on a deliberate angle, it makes the frame more dynamic and more bizarre. The more the characters became affected, the more the angle of the camera dipped"

Puppeteer Fiona Gentile has a bizarre memento of the episode. "I have Barry Otto's nose on my windowsill," she says. "When Rygel bites Doctor Tumii's nose off, I had to do this sleight of hand trick during the take. I brought Rygel's hand down, and slid the end of the nose off his glove with my own hand. I stuffed the nose into the pocket of my jeans, and a few days later, after my jeans had been through the wash, my husband came up to me holding this thing and asked me what the hell it was!" ∎

Opposite page: Dr Tumii pleads innocence

Above: Aeryn, Crichton and D'Argo have an unusual consultation with the doctor.

UNREALIZED REALITY

Written by: David Kemper	Guest cast: Lani Tupu (Crais), David Franklin (Braca),
Directed by: Andrew Prowse	John Bach (Einstein), Virginia Hey (Zhaan), Paul Goddard (Stark), Tammy MacIntosh (Jool), Murray Bartlett (DK)

Crichton is space walking outside Moya when a wormhole opens nearby, and to everyone's horror, extends and sucks him in. He spins wildly through it, eventually slamming through the wall. When he regains consciousness, he finds himself on an iceberg surrounded by black water, in some form of limbo. An interdimensional being, which Crichton names Einstein, appears before him in humanoid form. The being has been tracking Crichton, and was responsible for the wormhole that captured Moya some time earlier. He has summoned Crichton to discover why a human has been entrusted with wormhole knowledge. He tells Crichton of the way in which wormholes bridge space-time, providing the opportunity to affect the outcome of events. But when he discovers Crichton's wormhole knowledge has brought him to the attention of other species who would use it for their own ends, he tells the human that he will have to die...

> ### Rygel to Pilot
>
> "I wouldn't have risen to Dominar if I wasn't good at recognising things before they happen."
>
> "You were deposed in a coup led by your own cousin."

"'Unrealized Reality' is essentially David Kemper's vision of the world," Ben Browder maintains, "a billion different ideas." Kemper agrees. "For one episode, I put some theories out there," he says. "I had this theory of Unrealized Reality — the permutations of life are so myriad, and so interconnected to everything that is out there. I don't believe in predestination — that would be boring."

Although 'Unrealized Reality' is a roller-coaster ride, it was actually a money saving exercise. "We had to do an episode that shaved a day or two off the schedule," Kemper recalls. "We had one new guest star, and one new set. It needed minimal CG — just a wormhole and a laser blast. We threw some of the money we saved at the Creature Shop and decided to make it a physical production."

"Very early in the season," Tim Ferrier recalls, "David ripped the front cover off a *New Scientist* magazine showing an iceberg with three turrets on it, and told me it was the set for episode eleven. He knew then that Crichton's confrontation with this character would be a seminal point in the season."

Director Andrew Prowse had the challenging task of realising the different realities. "David writes cool sequences," Ben Browder notes, "The dif-

ficulty sometimes is integrating all the cool stuff that he writes. Andrew, working in conjunction with David, seems to find the best ways to do that. What he did in the edit became an almost associative style of film-making. He was pulling clips from the future, the past and out of thin air! He did an amazing job, and John Bach was tremendous, delivering very difficult exposition over long periods of time. His presence and ability was really the unifying force in that episode."

Above: Rygel/Noranti and Chiana/Aeryn on the alternate Moya's Command.

Next page: The human/Scarran hybrids of John Crichton and his father.

The Creature Shop had fun with new versions of familiar characters. Anthony Simcoe jokes that he wanted to play Jool because "I wanted breasts, OK? Jool is so different from D'Argo, plus I thought I wasn't going to be under so many prosthetics. But the costume was so uncomfortable that by the end of that couple of days shooting, I was praying to go back into the D'Argo make-up!"

"There were aliens running left, right and centre, getting tips off other aliens," Gigi Edgley recalls. "It was bizarre seeing another Chiana prancing about. I gained even more respect for the prosthetic characters and the Creature Shop after playing Noranti. It was a very intense feeling — people speak to you differently, and you hold yourself in a different way."

"The most horrifying element of that episode was the costume depart-

ment assuming I'd be able to fit into Gigi's costume!" Claudia Black says. "It took a while for them to refine her costume so that it was wearable for *her*, and they didn't have the same amount of time for me, so I just had to get into it and shoot."

Raelee Hill normally did all her own stunts, but let her double do the run across the wall when Sikozu is fleeing Peacekeeper Captain Crichton. "That was the only one I didn't do," she admits. "We only had one lot of glass, and it was very expensive. I was terrified of screwing it up!"

Ben Browder didn't relish the prospect of diving onto a concrete floor to recreate the fight in the cell from the première episode, but sustained a real injury when Black, as Chiana, jumped into his arms. "I bent his finger back when I jumped onto him," Black winces. "I was just devastated — he's taken so many wounds from that show, and I'm always distraught when I'm in any way responsible for them!" "You can hear the snap in the rough cut," Browder remembers. "But, hey, a couple of times a year I would get something like that!"

Filming the documentary sections triggered an idea in David Kemper's fertile mind: "I got everyone together and said it was so much fun to see people talking about Crichton, we had to do a documentary with our people and 'real' people. That was the genesis of the documentary episode, 'A Constellation of Doubt'." ■

Written by: Justin Monjo Directed by: Rowan Woods	Guest cast: Kent McCord (Jack Crichton), Rebecca Riggs (Grayza), David Franklin (Braca), Carmen Duncan (Leslie Crichton), Jamie Croft (Young John Crichton), Amy Salas (Skreeth)

Crichton's final journey through the wormhole has brought him into Earth orbit, and he manages to contact Moya. Sikozu and Scorpius remain on board the Leviathan, while the rest of the crew, in Lo'La, travel through a wormhole to rescue Crichton. When he listens to a radio broadcast, Crichton realises it is 1985, and that there's likely to be an upset in the time continuum. When they land in his hometown, Crichton is horrified to learn that contrary to history, his father Jack is slated to fly the doomed *Challenger* space shuttle mission. Crichton knows he must stop this, and hides his friends in a local abandoned house (luckily, the next day is Halloween, which means they might be able to remain anonymous). Crichton tries to talk to his younger self, but realises there is nothing the younger Crichton could say that would prevent his father from taking the mission...

Crichton

"Y'all might want to stay out of sight. We don't want to screw up the universe any more than I already have."

"'Kansas' was the best script I had in the fourth season," director Rowan Woods says firmly. "Justin Monjo trod a tightrope with the tone. You had the fairly gratuitous *Munsters*-style story of our guys in the house on planet Earth at Halloween, and then in stark contrast there was the intense melancholy of Crichton coming home."

David Kemper had decided it was time that John Crichton got back to Earth, but in typical *Farscape* fashion it wouldn't be in the way the audience expected. "Everyone hears the main titles, but nobody listens to them," he explains. "John Crichton wants to go home — so how can we not give him what he wants? The original concept was that Crichton would never go back to Earth, but I wanted to use Dad, and really mine some emotion. The initial plan was to do a two-parter. In the first hour we'd go back to Halloween 1972 when Crichton's about six years old, and then go to the present day."

In Justin Monjo's script, the date changed to the mid-1980s, not long before the space shuttle *Challenger* exploded during its ascent. 'Kansas' uses the actual footage of the *Challenger*'s final moments. "I thought that was an incredibly confronting and brave thing to do," Rowan Woods says. "We'd never taken a tragic historic event and portrayed it for what it was." "We played the story about Crichton, rather than on the tragedy itself,"

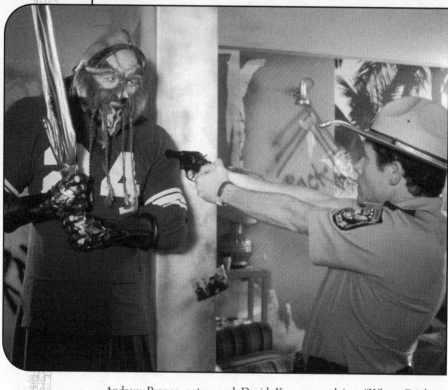

Andrew Prowse notes, and David Kemper explains, "When Crichton realises his Dad's going to be on the *Challenger*, he has a visual memory in his head. We're showing a flash of his memory, and the show always has to be from Crichton's point of view."

Kent McCord dyed his hair for his first appearance this season. "Jack is a hardass, at odds with his son," he notes. "John's going through the pain of the teenage years, so Jack wants to do what's best for him. Being a father of three grown children, this is all part of my own background! The scenes were so well written, they played themselves."

Tim Ferrier recreated 1985 Florida in the Sydney suburb of Sylvania Waters. "We found a nice house, then wrecked it, emptied the pool and made it grotty, much to the chagrin of the owners," the production designer jokes. The real-life owner of the stunt car wasn't impressed with D'Argo's antics behind the wheel. "We had to do so many takes with D'Argo backing the car out of the driveway and crashing into the rubbish bins," Anthony Simcoe recalls. "The poor guy was tearing his hair out watching me!" Simcoe enjoyed the location work for the Earth episodes. "Imagine suburban Sydney locals watching all these weird characters

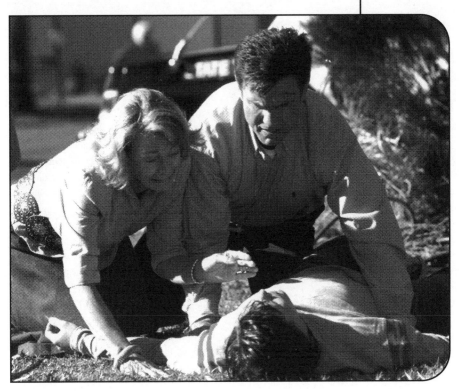

jumping around," he laughs, and Gigi Edgley adds, "The neighbours think it's quite intriguing seeing aliens tromping down their streets, half made-up, with a cigarette hanging out of their mouths. You should have seen the look on the early morning joggers' faces!"

"It was freezing cold," Claudia Black remembers. "Up until then, we'd been having a bit of an Indian summer, but you can't predict when the weather is going to turn. And turn it did!" Black thinks it was a shame that after Aeryn had spent so long learning English during the previous episodes, the others picked it up so quickly. "It made her look retarded!" she says. "It took her so long, and suddenly everyone else is basically fluent. How else can Chiana communicate enough to be able to have a relationship with the young Crichton? It was worth it though, because that was a very sinister twist to know that John lost his virginity to Chiana!" "Chi had the time of her life," Gigi Edgley giggles. "She had her very own Crichton!" Ben Browder was delighted by the performance of his younger self. "Jamie Croft did a really lovely job," he says.

"It's about Crichton's feeling of never being able to go home," David Kemper concludes. "Justin and Rowan worked so well together, hand in glove. It was a stylised, brilliant episode." ■

Opposite page: D'Argo faces the Sheriff.

Above: Leslie and Jack Crichton help their injured son.

TERRA FIRMA

Written by: Richard Manning
Directed by: Peter Andrikidis

Guest cast: Kent McCord (Jack Crichton), Rebecca Riggs (Grayza), David Franklin (Braca), Murray Bartlett (DK), Geoff Morell (Holt), Katherine Thomas (Laura), Erica Heynatz (Caroline), Amy Salas (Skreeth)

he crew returns to Moya in orbit around Earth in late 2003 to find Jack Crichton and a contingent of dignitaries from Earth waiting for them. Initially suspicious, Crichton soon accepts he has finally been reunited with his father. The crew is soon introduced to an amazed and apprehensive public. Aeryn makes every effort to learn Crichton's home customs and language, hoping to reconcile with him, but he seems oblivious, relying on Noranti's medication to keep her from his mind. He is more concerned with the progress of Earth's scientists, who want information on wormhole technology that he is not prepared to give them. Worse still, Jack sides with the government in opposition to Crichton's wish to share the knowledge with *all* nations, not just the USA. Meanwhile, Grayza's monstrous assassin, the Skreeth, makes its way to Earth...

> ### Sikozu to Crichton
>
> "What is wrong with you? These are your people. Or do you think they pose us a threat?"
>
> "No, it's the other way around."

"'Terra Firma' is a *huge* turning point in the series for Crichton," writer Ricky Manning points out. "What does it mean for him to be on Earth? He's not the same John Crichton who left, and it's not time for him to come home yet. There's too much other stuff going on out there. He's got two powerful, aggressive species after him, not to mention each other. He's in the middle of these two giant wrecking balls on a collision course. He wants to be as far from Earth as possible at this moment, yet it's somewhere that he's been aspiring to be for so long."

Ben Browder describes 'Terra Firma' as "one of my favourite episodes of the year, and of the series. It takes a humongous risk. 'Space series go to Earth to die', you know. We went there four times!" It was Browder's idea to use a voiceover. "Initially he was saying that to camera," director Peter Andrikidis recalls, "but Ben thought of the voiceover, and it gave the episode a downbeat

ENCOUNTERS: SKREETH

An extremely deadly, green-hued, cat-like creature with an in-built camouflage mechanism: an invisibility shroud that's activated when the creature remains completely motionless. The Skreeth can communicate telepathically via a symbiotic relationship with a larnapse, which is placed on the skull of a third party, enabling communication even over huge distances.

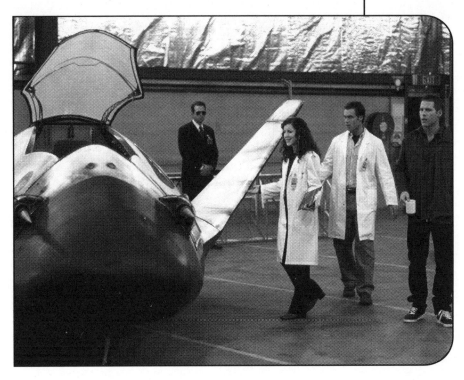

resonance." "It gave me leeway to adjust it as we were going along," Browder explains. "In my mind it's more an *Apocalypse Now*-type voiceover."

"From a musical point of view, that scene on the dock is a summary of where we are going with the episode," Guy Gross notes. "So I scored it with a slightly melancholy, reflective piece of music, almost in *On Golden Pond* style. It shows John's dilemma — happiness on one side, sadness on the other."

The voiceover and jump of a few weeks between the opening scene and the first act "meant we skipped past *The Day the Earth Stood Still* stuff with humans reacting to the aliens, and got straight to the emotion," Ricky Manning says. "It's so easy to have fun with aliens on Earth, but Justin did such a lovely job of that in 'Kansas'."

"Three weeks earlier, you're on a spaceship with farting puppets and women peeing in buckets," Ben Browder comments, "and in 'Terra Firma' we had a scene with a father and son having a domestic argument about politics, that could be in a movie of the week somewhere!"

The Skreeth may have brought destruction to Earth, but "I always felt that the Skreeth was somebody who Grayza liked," Rebecca Riggs says. "She had far more respect and liking for the Skreeth than she did for Braca, that's for sure!"

Above: DK and Laura examine Crichton's module.

Next page: The Skreeth prepares to attack DK.

"The whole concept I had for the episode was *A Farscape Christmas*," David Kemper recalls. "We were going to do Christmas the *Farscape* way — you know, blow the crap out of everything." Although originally the production team had hoped to be able to destroy an actual house, this wasn't feasible, and Tim Ferrier built a set specifically to be torn apart in the firefight between Crichton, Aeryn and the Skreeth. "Peter Andrikidis is a very seasoned director," Ferrier says. "That fight couldn't have gone better. I was on set and it looked terrific." "We destroyed an entire house," Browder smiles. "Merry Frelling Christmas!"

The fight with the Skreeth had a serious purpose. "I liked the fact we took no prisoners in this episode," Claudia Black comments, while David Kemper explains, "Crichton realises that this is what *one* creature can do on his planet — it's killed his friends! Does he really want to bring the universe back to Earth? It shows him beyond a shadow of a doubt that he can't allow this to happen."

"The key to Crichton's emotional journey was getting the last scene between him and his father right," director Andrikidis notes. "His dad has got him back, but he's got to go, because he's brought back all those weapons." ■

Written by: David Peckinpah	Guest cast: Paula Arundell (Talikaa), Chris Pitman
Directed by: Kate Woods	(Nazradu), Walter Grkovic (Outurak)

Noranti and Rygel buy maps of Tormented Space from traders led by the grim Nazradu. The traders offer something else for sale before they leave — an abused girl in their possession, named Talikaa. At Chiana's insistence, the crew agrees to buy her. But Talikaa has a strange effect on those she meets. Aeryn becomes colder than usual to Crichton, and then prevents Chiana and Talikaa from getting too close. D'Argo is furious with Rygel when he learns that the Dominar gave the traders counterfeit krendars, while the Hynerian becomes greedier than usual, and Crichton starts to get even more optimistic. After Scorpius interrupts Chiana trying to push Crichton into having sex with her, he points out to Crichton that everyone is behaving abnormally. But the obvious cause of the problem, Talikaa, has disappeared from her quarters, and when Crichton and Aeryn try to find her, they are attacked by a huge spider…

Crichton

"I know you can see me. Bad guys always see me. My plans suck. People die. It's always a mess."

"I thought Kate Woods did a good job with that episode," producer Andrew Prowse says of the director débuting on 'Twice Shy'. "It's a solid story, with solid performances."

Although Woods hadn't directed anything of this nature before, she admits she was "bitten by sci-fi" as a result of the experience. "I never worried about it being a ship-bound episode," she says. "I thought it was a great chance to get back to the relationships between the characters in their home environments. I wanted to embrace the smallness of it, and make that a plus. We could get into the depths of characterisation, which is where I am most comfortable as a director. We could explore extremes of emotion, and how each character would move in their extreme."

ENCOUNTERS: WOLAXIAN ARACHNID

Found throughout Tormented Space, this race takes the form of both a Sebacean and a spider-like creature. Its touch in the Sebacean form infects the victim, stimulating exaggerated neural functioning. In its arachnid form, the creature can harvest the energy from its victim, storing it in membrane orbs and hiding those orbs in an external nest for later consumption. This process leaves the victims completely drained and close to death.

When more time was needed to construct the sets for 'Terra Firma', 'Twice Shy' was moved ahead in the production order. "David Peckinpah is a consummate professional," David Kemper says. "He didn't have a lot of time to write this to start with, and then he lost seven days!"

Although this meant that the cast were more reliant than usual on the director to guide them through the story on set, it did give them a chance to experiment. "The actors are so in tune with the whole world of the show," Woods comments. "They added an enormous amount. It was a very organic process. I've always been very nervous of that, because I've always wanted to go in with a tight script, but on *Farscape* it worked very well not to. We could develop things all the time on the studio floor."

"From an acting standpoint, episodes like this are difficult," Ben Browder comments. "The emotions are generated by a mystical outside force. You're playing a generalised state — Crichton is bitten, and wakes up 'happy', or 'depressed'. As an actor, you normally play a specific state, but here we were having to do what is generally considered bad acting!" Claudia Black agrees: "It's a technical device. You can't deliver any real emotion, because everything's been exaggerated. It's difficult to be sincere and keep the line of the story going when you're constantly having to indicate a heightened state."

The improvisational aspect of the episode was assisted by the casting of noted Australian actress Paula Arundell as Talikaa. The production team had previously considered her for the parts of Neeyala in 'Wait for the Wheel', and Commandant Grayza. "I really wanted to use her, because she's such a fantastic and incredibly capable theatre actress," Andrew Prowse says. "I stuck my neck out to make it happen, and I'm glad I did." "Paula was terrific," Woods adds. "She dived into this head first!"

Gigi Edgley "really liked the connection Chiana had with Talikaa when she first came on board. I found the first scene when you see the two of them alone really bizarre. It was hard to surrender to the words in this one, so I decided to play it as if Chi was entranced by Queen Mab entering the building."

The post-production team had their work cut out for them, thanks to the computer-generated spider. "The whole notion of CG creatures went to another level this season," Deb Peart says. "You've got to be very careful how you use them though, because you don't want to give too much, and risk seeing their imperfections." That fitted in with David Kemper's ideas. "We wanted a spooky episode," he says. "You don't know what's hiding in the shadows. We played it as a mystery, and Kate did a great job realising it all." ■

Opposite page: Crichton surrenders to Talikaa's power.

Above: *Chiana threatens to kill Talikaa rather than let her stay a slave.*

MENTAL AS ANYTHING

Written by: Mark Saraceni	Guest cast: Blair Venn (Macton), John Brumpton
Directed by: Geoff Bennett	(Katoya), Rachel Gordon (Lo'Laan)

n exchange for information about the creature that attacked Crichton and Aeryn on Earth, Scorpius signs up D'Argo, Rygel and a dubious Crichton for a technologically advanced training camp where students are taught mental discipline. The compound is run by Master Katoya, an alien of formidable power, whose students battle each other mentally in cyberspace. Macton, the Peacekeeper who killed D'Argo's wife, Lo'Laan, and framed him for the murder, is also a student in training. Breaching compound regulations, the enraged D'Argo attacks Macton, but is quickly restrained by Katoya, and told that further transgressions are punishable by death. Macton wastes no time trying to persuade Crichton that it was the Luxan who killed his wife, in a fit of Hyperrage. Crichton refuses to believe him, but is surprised by D'Argo's reaction. Knowing that Hyperrage causes blackouts and memory loss, D'Argo begins to suspect he may have murdered his own wife after all...

Katoya to D'Argo

"What would you like to know?"

"What kind of monster I really am."

"I was presented with a problem," David Kemper recalls. "Throughout the season, we constantly look ahead at the schedule, and we realised that the actors had so much ADR [additional dialogue recording, in post-production] to do, we couldn't finish the episodes. We had a delivery timetable to the network, and we couldn't meet that unless the actors were freed up. So I decided we would do one episode with all the boys, and one with all the girls."

Earlier in the season, there had been a discussion about when the time would be right to deal with D'Argo's backstory, and whether it might wait until season five or possibly even season six. But following the *Farscape* policy of 'play the card', they decided to go ahead and discover what had happened to Macton straight away.

"Mark Saraceni had this brilliant idea of finding out that D'Argo isn't perfect," Kemper says. "He smacked his wife once. It had such an emotional edge to it, and we had to be really careful that we pulled it off properly, and didn't make the episode too goofy. Justin Monjo was going for the tough line, and saying that D'Argo really *did* kill his wife, as Macton claims. I didn't know if we wanted to go that far. I felt we still had to like the characters, and I wanted to be sure that we didn't disservice D'Argo."

Andrew Prowse recalls this as "the D'Argo episode of the year. It had to be all about D'Argo. It's about him wrestling with his demons. It wasn't

about Crichton doing whatever he was doing in his little hellhole, it was about D'Argo!"

Anthony Simcoe worked closely with director Geoff Bennett to achieve the emotional layering that the script demanded. "They were more like emotional colours than anything else," Simcoe says. "We wanted to make sure we got the intensity of the emotions in. It was a real moment for me of just digging down into a deep emotional space, which I found really enjoyable."

Composer Guy Gross found it "challenging to express D'Argo's pain, so we could really understand his story. I allowed the doubt to stay in my mind and I didn't want to resolve D'Argo's dilemma musically until right at the end, when we knew what the answer was."

For the flashback sequences, "we wanted to go back to D'Argo's season one make-up," Simcoe recalls. "But the practicalities of shooting the show on the schedule that we had would have meant a complete make-up change for me in mid-flow, which would have taken nearly five hours! They were such small scenes that it just wasn't practical, unfortunately."

Kemper is also pleased that the story also focuses attention on Rygel, who fights valiantly against the hated Charrid. "He really is a brave guy,"

Above: Katoya readies his students for their next tutorial.

Next page: D'Argo and Lo'Laan ponder their future.

he points out. "He doesn't know how good, and how strong he actually is until he's confronted. He's learned he's got this in him: it's kind of dawned on him over time. Because he's a little bit of a wanker, frankly, people don't listen to him as much as they should, but ultimately he's the smartest guy on the ship!"

The icasahedron in which the battles were fought caused a few practical problems on set. "When you were on the studio floor," Ben Browder recalls, "the set was just lights, and the opening of a CG area. When you worked in it, you got motion sickness, because whenever you turned your head, the lights moved — but you weren't moving!"

"The ball inside cyberspace was a huge undertaking for visual effects," Deb Peart recalls. "A lot of time was spent making sure that all the moves were right. It seemed simple, but it wasn't. There's only so much time you can spend watching a growing ball moving from one direction to another."

"Mark tackled an episode that had lots of layers to it," Kemper concludes, "and did a really good job. Anthony did brilliantly, giving us the emotion of the show. D'Argo finally gets his revenge, but we find out that he wasn't without guilt." ■

BRINGING HOME THE BEACON

Written by: Carleton Eastlake	**Guest cast:** Francesca Buller (Ahkna), John Pasvolsky
Directed by: Rowan Woods	(Pennoch), Peter Lamb (Rekka), Peter Fenton
	(Negotiator), Olivia Pigeot (Marella)

On a commerce settlement formed from the fusion of a dead Leviathan and an asteroid, Moya's female crewmembers make a deal for a sensor distorter that will protect Moya from long-range scans. While they are waiting for the necessary modifications to be made, Aeryn and Sikozu witness the arrival of a Peacekeeper contingent led by Grayza and Braca. Soon after, a squad of Scarran emissaries land, led by Ahkna, their insidious Minister of War. Chiana and Noranti become separated from the others, and are forced to hide from the Peacekeeper commandos. Their only chance to escape undetected is to undergo genetic manipulation to change their appearance. Aeryn and Sikozu spy on the meeting and overhear Grayza offering to trade control of the Luxan worlds for peace in the Uncharted Territories. Aeryn realises that Grayza must be stopped, and decides to assassinate the treacherous Peacekeeper Commandant, no matter what it takes...

> ### Sikozu to Chiana
>
> "Wait, Chiana, please. For once in your life, exercise some self-control."
>
> "I am exercising self-control. I'm not blasting off your head."

"'Bringing Home the Beacon' was an intense little piece, with our girls separated from the boys," Rowan Woods recalls. "We were getting a lot of information and story together, and at its dramatic heart was the introduction of Ahkna, which was very impressive. A lot of magnificent creatures were suddenly in our faces!" Ahkna was portrayed by Francesca Buller, returning to play her fourth character on the show. "I wanted it to look as if this was a one-off appearance," David Kemper says, "but we already knew Ahkna was coming back at the end of the year."

Buller was delighted with the role: "She was described as being the Minister of War, extremely clever at playing political games, very stoic and desperate to succeed by her own mettle." She was inspired by her costume, created by fabrication designer Lou Elsey. "Lou took me to the House of Fetish,"

ENCOUNTERS: BIOLOID

A genetically engineered bio-mechanical replication of a living creature. This process is used extensively by the Scarrans to supplant their enemies in the Peacekeeper hierarchy. Kalish Bioloids have the ability to transform into weapons designed to overload Scarran heat glands.

Buller recalls, "and I tried on these boots that went right to the top of my thighs, with two inch heels. There's no way you can be timid in those! I had a corset as well, and once I had the rest of the costume, I also looked at the Cate Blanchett film *Elizabeth*, and various science fiction roles, including *Star Trek*'s Borg Queen."

"Fran *owned* that role," Woods says. "She had played a couple of fantabulous characters on *Farscape* who had been frittery and jerky, but this time she was regal — a selfish, screwed up version of the Queen. She was born to rule, and vicious to boot!"

Ahkna and Grayza made a lethal combination. "We were two women in control!" Buller says, while Rebecca Riggs "adored working with Fran. We weren't aware there was so much exposition though: when you watch the scenes between Ahkna and Grayza, the focus is actually Aeryn and Sikozu hearing the information and making decisions based on it."

Gigi Edgley enjoyed a chance to experiment with a different look. "We workshopped that quite extensively," she recalls. "After the first test, I went on set and nobody recognised me. I liked that, but it didn't meld with Chiana's look enough — we put in green contacts, and my hair was halfway down my back."

"Ben completely reinvented the scene at the end," Rowan Woods reveals. "He created a tense piece that had a Pinter-like quality to it. For a second you think Crichton has lost it." "We never quite solved the problem of how Crichton knew about 'Aeryn' being a Bioloid," Browder admits, "but I decided it was a gut reaction thing. Crichton knows her on a level that goes beyond the physical."

"I find that confrontation really unsettling," Woods admits. "I think the prosthetic piece Dave Elsey came up with is exquisite. There are one or two shots I find quite hard to look at. I didn't expect to be able to hold on those shots as long as I did, but the prosthetic just holds up beautifully."

"We were going to try to mix make-up, animatronics, puppets and real people, and CG them together in a beautiful blend," Dave Elsey recalls. "The plan was to stick a prosthetic on the actor, with a green screen area so post-production could add the CG 'mechanics'. Then it would look as if half her face was missing. Unfortunately, Claudia developed an allergy to the prosthetic, so we had to make a fake head, and filled it with valves, bladders and tripe — which Rowan couldn't stop filming!"

"I think this was Dave Elsey's finest year," David Kemper says. "He did some spectacular stuff along the way. It was above and beyond fantastic — it was outrageously good!" ∎

Opposite page:
Noranti gets Sikozu out of trouble.

Above: *The DNA-altered Noranti and Chiana.*

Written by: David Kemper	Guest cast: Nick Tate (R. Wilson Monroe), Sarah Enright
Directed by: Andrew Prowse	(Olivia Crichton), Joshua Anderson (Bobby Coleman)

ith Aeryn in the Scarrans' hands, Crichton is at his wits' end. He is unable to sleep, and obsessed with a television transmission that Pilot has intercepted from Earth: a documentary about the visitation by "aliens" — Moya's crew. Sikozu is trying to locate Katratzi, where she believes Aeryn has been taken, but can find no reference to it. The *Alien Visitation* documentary is based on various analyses of videotape of Moya's crew taken by Crichton's nephew Bobby while they were on Earth. The more he watches it, the more Crichton realises that Earth is simply not ready to encounter the rest of the galaxy's life forms. Everything that any of his friends said has been taken out of context, and given the most sinister possible connotation. However, nothing that any of the rest of the crew can say will distract him from this last connection with his home planet...

Rygel

" It's a backward planet full of superstitious, xenophobic morons. Nothing makes sense if they didn't think of it first, and even then it's simplistic drivel."

"I knew that episode seventeen was going to be different," David Kemper says. "I invited everyone to give me their thoughts. I realised our crew had been on modern day Earth for all of 'Terra Firma', and I wondered what else happened. They didn't just sit around! When I saw the documentary footage shot for 'Unrealized Reality', I knew that was the way to show it. The real purpose of 'A Constellation of Doubt' was to service Crichton finding the clue to saving Aeryn," he continues, "but as a writer I was able to slide some things in about someone looking at Earth for the first time."

"Kemper turned into a writing machine and wrote some really cool stuff," Ben Browder notes. "A lot of it was discarded, but it was all entertaining and interesting." "The script for this episode is legendary," Andrew Prowse adds. "It was collated two days *after* we finished shooting it!"

Cast and crew are full of admiration for guest star Nick Tate's role as documentary host R. Wilson Monroe, who Kemper likened to veteran American newscaster Walter Cronkite. "You could give that man his own show," Andrew Prowse says. "You could believe he was that slightly pompous, terribly serious interviewer."

There are two moments in the episode that give Kemper chills to watch. "The first is when Crichton figures out where he heard the name 'Katratzi', and realises that he can find Aeryn," he explains, "That was probably the finest scene of the year. Ben and Raelee were on fire. The

other moment is when R. Wilson Monroe asks Aeryn if the two species can procreate, and Aeryn freezes. Claudia did such a great job there!"

The scene where Crichton throws Rygel out of his cell caused some problems on set. "Rygel is sitting eating a big bowl of popcorn," Fiona Gentile recalls, "and Ben upturned it all over Rygel. Rygel's mouth had been open, and got stuffed full of popcorn. Suddenly he couldn't open or shut his mouth! We had to try to deliver the line, but none of us knew how to fix it. Mat McCoy very sheepishly waddled Rygel off!"

The episode was shot in chunks. Part of the documentary footage was filmed on location during the shooting of 'Terra Firma', and the sequences on Moya were filmed after 'Prayer'. However, the rest of the documentary footage was filmed at the end of the year. "This was the episode we were filming when we learned the show had been cancelled," Andrew Prowse notes.

In fact, the very last scene to be filmed on the series was Crichton and Olivia's discussion of Crichton's "tell" in the Maintenance Bay. "We started that on Take 33," Browder recalls. "Anthony Simcoe is fond of say-

Above: Sikozu tries to locate Katratzi.

Next page: R. Wilson Monroe quizzes Bobby Coleman on the set of Alien Visitation.

ing, 'Second takes are for dickheads — but Take 33: Brando!' So we started this slate on Take 33. I was hoping to get it in one, but we went to Take 36."

"At the very end, there was a bit about how the *Farscape* project had been betrayed," Andrew Prowse recalls. "So the very last words we shot were: '*Farscape* has died'."

'A Constellation of Doubt' was one of Deb Peart's favourite episodes of the season. "It was huge," she recalls. "When Nick Holmes cut it together, the first assembly was two hours long, if we put every expert opinion in there. We had to create the *Alien Visitation* programme as well," she adds. "We had to make the transitions and captions work, and make sure the names we'd given to the experts didn't actually belong to any real people!"

"We got a lot of resistance to this episode," David Kemper recalls. "Certain people couldn't understand how we could make a 'documentary episode'. But I'm glad we held to our lines. Like it or hate it, this episode saw us taking risks, setting up the rest of the year, and giving us a breath of fresh air before the roller-coaster of intensity in the final episodes." ■

PRAYER

Written by: Justin Monjo **Directed by:** Peter Andrikidis	**Guest cast:** Jason Clarke (Jenek), Sandy Gore (Vreena), Sacha Horler (Morrock)

eryn is being held captive aboard a Scarran freighter captained by Jenek, a ruthless and ambitious Scarran of the Ruling Order, who is trying to find out where Crichton is. On Moya, Crichton makes a deal with Scorpius, reinforced by a Scarran Blood Vow: if Scorpius helps him rescue Aeryn, Crichton will finally give him the wormhole knowledge he wants so badly. Jenek and a traitorous Sebacean nurse, Vreena, question Aeryn, forcing her to battle against powerful drugs and searing Scarran heat torture. Crichton navigates his way through the wormholes to the alternate reality he visited courtesy of Einstein, where the Banik version of Sikozu mentioned the name Katratzi. Meanwhile, Jenek is keen to increase Aeryn's torture, but Vreena stops him when she discovers that Aeryn is pregnant. They realise they no longer need to capture Crichton to obtain the wormhole knowledge. If the child is Crichton's, they can extract all the answers they need from the foetus's DNA...

> ### Scorpius to Crichton
>
> "Why is nothing ever easy with you?"
>
> "I wish I knew."

"Justin wanted to do a harsh, hard episode, that was tough to deal with," David Kemper says. "It was a very contained show, and one that gave Claudia a lot to do. Justin likes writing for her, and together they brought it home." "Claudia really went for it!" Peter Andrikidis remembers. "It was a pretty full-on episode. It was very focused, without too many visual effects. I prefer that kind of character-based, intense episode."

Claudia Black would actually have liked the end result to have been even more extreme than what ended up on screen. "I didn't want it to be an absurd melodrama, where the audience would know that they were being taken on a roller-coaster ride," she explains. "It needed some legitimacy and some weight to it. But a lot of the more grotesque torture sequences were taken out."

'Prayer' is an unusual episode, as the person driving the story is totally inactive. "That's such a difficult conundrum to deal with," Black notes. "Aeryn was tied to a bed! She's using her mind and her words to manipulate the situation, but she's incapacitated. It's very hard to be the lead protagonist when you've got probes in you, and you're writhing around, frothing at the mouth. In the end, you just start to use different parts of your body. You go with what you're given. It was all so difficult, given the constraints of the episode. She's being tortured throughout. Nothing really happens — she can't escape, and she's being drugged!"

Black also knew that the audience could be led to believe Aeryn's stories of other lovers, because she had deliberately kept an air of mystery about Aeryn's time away from the ship between seasons. "What she reveals in her hazed state could potentially still be possible," she points out. "It was strange after all these years of Crichton having loads of affairs and Aeryn being true to her man, that we suddenly saw these sequences of her with other men. If there was going to be a love scene, I wanted it to be as tender and real as we could."

Tim Ferrier had the budget to create a large set for the cell, as it was going to be redressed for use in later episodes. "After tightening our belts for some considerable time, we loosened them a lot," he recalls. "One of my greatest pleasures on *Farscape* was designing torture implements! I presented the drawing of the torture bed for Claudia at the production meeting, and there was an awful silence until David said, 'This is really scary!' Claudia was a good sport and got into it. It wasn't that uncomfortable: the whole point is to make it *look* uncomfortable when it's not."

Peter Andrikidis was concerned that the scenes between Crichton and Scorpius in the alternate reality might jar with the dark nature of the Aeryn sequences. "So those became darker as well," he reveals. "Ben and

Wayne took those scenes to the limit."

The moment when Scorpius shoots Chiana/Aeryn in the alternate reality reinforces Scorpius as a villain. "It was important it was done that way," Browder notes. "It shows Scorpius's direct brutality. He's been withholding it from John, but now you see it back in evidence. He has a singular focus — and that's why Crichton went to him."

Browder also finds the "Scarran breeding program, using whatever species they can get their hands on, hard and repulsive." David Kemper initially was against showing the abortion, "but Justin pointed out that it's not real. That I could buy — as long as it's not real, and the audience realises we're tricking them, that's okay. We're a tough show."

"This episode was torturous, but it wasn't random or meaningless," Browder says. "It plays heavily into the series arc. Hopefully we didn't scare too many people off. But it's odd to think it's possible for us to scare an audience off by being too harsh, when there are shows like *Oz* and *The Sopranos* out there."

"The episode had a lot of surprises," Andrikidis says of his final directing stint. "We always tried to push right to the edge, but this time everyone was pushing to break the boundaries!" ■

Opposite page: Chiana/Aeryn and Stark/Sikozu face their captors.

Above: Jenek demands the truth from Aeryn.

WE'RE SO SCREWED
PART I: FETAL ATTRACTION

Written by: David Peckinpah	Guest cast: Jason Clarke (Jenek), Shane Briant (Trayso),
Directed by: Geoff Bennett	Sandy Gore (Vreena), Rel Hunt (Karohm), Patrick Ward
	(Ralnaht), Ben Dalton (Zepa)

Moya's crew arrives at a Scarran Border Station, where the freighter holding Aeryn is docked for inspection. Scorpius masquerades as a Scarran captain with the Ministry of Dissimulation, with Crichton, Chiana and Rygel posing as spies working for him. Sikozu has gone ahead of the rest of the crew, and ingratiated herself with her fellow Kalish, who act as bureaucrats on the station. She discovers that Aeryn's ship is due to leave for Katratzi in barely half an arn — insufficient time to stage a rescue. To keep the freighter at the station, Rygel feigns symptoms of the deadly disease known as Hynerian dermaphollica, forcing the base's Kalish medical officer, Trayso, to impose a lockdown. Noranti and D'Argo arrive and pose as medical experts. When Trayso starts to doubt the authenticity of the disease, Noranti gives Rygel the real thing. If she can't come up with a cure quickly, he will die...

> **Rygel to Chiana**
>
> "Sikozu thinks with her head, not her kuzitza."
>
> "Yeah, that's her problem."

"I have always wanted to call an episode 'We're So Screwed' ever since the moment in 'Look at the Princess' when Crichton is dancing around crazily in the Jakench cockpit with Braca going, 'We're so screwed, man!'" says Andrew Prowse. David Kemper adds, "It's also a reference to Crichton's predicament. And yes, it was a reference to *Farscape* being cancelled by the SCI FI Channel." The subtitle for this episode came from another suggestion by Prowse, superseding Ricky Manning's idea of 'Foetus, Don't Fail Me Now'!

"We were tired, and we ran out of time to make this episode more than it was," Kemper admits. "Sometimes you get caught. We had to shoot this in six

ENCOUNTERS: KALISH

Orange-hued, intelligent beings subjugated by the Scarrans into a lifetime of subservience. The Kalish have an incredible ability to assimilate information, making them invaluable advisors in all sorts of fields of interest. They can also shift their centre of gravity allowing them to walk on walls, and reattach their appendages if they are torn off.

days in order to make sure we had enough time to film the final three episodes. But David Peckinpah worked really hard on this, and it achieved what we wanted. Crichton desperately wants to go and rescue Aeryn, but he has to wait around for the right moment." "We're finally off to Scarranburg," Ben Browder says. "This is a linking episode. Everyone is doing their bits and pieces, and the crew is reasonably intact and functioning."

"I threaded the idea that Aeryn isn't sure whether the apparitions are real or not through the episode," Claudia Black recalls. "At the start, she's responding to what she thinks is Crichton, but then when that Crichton leaves, she doesn't trust the next one. When Noranti really is there, she doesn't trust her, and when Crichton does arrive, she refuses to trust that it's him. That earned the moment later on when she wakes up on Moya and asks if he is real. Aeryn wasn't really aware of what was going on when Crichton came to rescue her from the baby being taken."

"Originally Crichton was going to rescue Aeryn with Noranti there," Kemper recalls, "and Ben just came in and stared at me until I said, 'OK — just the hero saves the girl!' and then he smiled."

The episode does give a lot of attention to Noranti, and Rygel. "Rygel's Technicolor vomit was amazing to see on the set," Fiona Gentile recalls. "The special effects guys surpassed themselves. We had a lot of trouble rigging it, because we weren't sure if we could get a tube up through Rygel's neck, and in

Above: Scorpius tries to persuade Crichton to do things his way.

Next page: Jenek refuses to assist during the infection.

the end it came out of the side. He sprayed the entire set — it went on forever coming out red, pink and blue. They went through tons of dyed gelatine!"

Mat McCoy also had a challenging time portraying the sick Hynerian. "We had a really good scene with Noranti," he says. "She's telling him that he probably won't die, but could, and Rygel is freaking out. We got some really nice action into that, as if he's scratching away maniacally at his neck. It was really hard to do, but it was well worth it because it really sold the idea he was covered in hives."

"The end of the episode has one of the great performances of *Farscape*," Ben Browder maintains, "with Wayne Pygram as Nosferatu. I liked the fact we were bringing back the very first pop reference that Crichton ever called Scorpius. Wayne thought his performance might be too big, but I thought it was spot on."

"I came in on the second day of colour-grading the film," Deb Peart recalls, "and told Andrew I was going to play around with that last sequence, and make it look like a 1920s movie. We took all the colour out, and then added some scratches to it, and some shifts to the movement. It's the sort of thing that removes *Farscape* from normal television." ■

WE'RE SO SCREWED
PART II: HOT TO KATRATZI

Written by: Carleton Eastlake	Guest cast: Paul Goddard (Stark), Rebecca Riggs
Directed by: Karl Zwicky	(Grayza), David Franklin (Braca), Duncan Young (Staleek),
	Francesca Buller (Ahkna), Jason Clarke (Jenek)

oya's crew travels to Katratzi to stop the Scarrans from torturing wormhole information out of Scorpius. They arrive during critical peace negotiations between Commandant Grayza and the Scarran Emperor, Staleek. To discourage reprisals against the crew, Crichton wears a nuclear bomb, rigged to explode should anything happen to him. He claims to have come to the base to sell wormhole knowledge to the highest bidder, causing both sides to try to do a deal with him, although the Scarrans also begin working out a way to disable the bomb. While D'Argo and Rygel create unrest amongst the Charrids stationed on Katratzi, Sikozu uses her connections with the Kalish resistance to undermine security. In doing so, she sends Crichton and Aeryn to a top-secret part of the base, an area of vital importance to Scarran domination. Ahkna continues her torture of Scorpius, and brings in an unexpected ally to assist with the interrogation — the Banik, Stark...

> **Aeryn to Rygel**
>
> "We're going to walk into the most heavily guarded base in the Scarran Empire, start a civil war and walk out with Scorpius. What part of that do you not understand?"

"I can't think of another show that would attempt the number of pros- thetic and animatronic characters we had in the big scene at the beginning of that episode," novice *Farscape* director Karl Zwicky maintains. "Just to get them all on set took hours, and we had them all in one shot!"

"'Hot to Katratzi' was all about bringing in the Scarrans who were going to be the villains for the fifth year," David Kemper points out. "In my world, the only way you can introduce villains properly is to have a scene where they are formidable, and our hero is formidable. That's why we had the great sequence at the start where Crichton jumps on the table. And our new vil- lains have friction from the first minute, which we would have continued in the fifth season."

"The writing staff came up with this stupendous scene," Ben Browder comments, "and we did four takes with Crichton yakking away. I wondered how I was going to pull it off. I knew there was going to be a room full of peo- ple, most of whom I didn't know because they were playing new characters, and I was going to make a complete pranny of myself."

Browder adlibbed the line 'I am an American', "and I was so tempted

to play the American national anthem in the score when he said that," Guy Gross reveals. "But I thought that might alienate the rest of the world, so I just wrote a few reasonably patriotic bars underneath that."

"I liked the fact this episode had such a strong central story to it," Karl Zwicky says. "Our hero has an atomic bomb strapped to him! In one of our endless five-hour story conferences, I told David that I was very happy with this core story. All the rest of the strands had the complexity that *Farscape* is famous for, but at its base it had a very simple idea."

Some of those strands included the Charrid-Kalish civil war that Crichton sends D'Argo, Rygel and Sikozu out to foment. "There was a terrific little fight which they shot in no time at all," Andrew Prowse notes, while Gigi Edgley adds that "all the fight scenes in this episode with Chiana were tweaked because of the shooting schedules. I would have loved to have taken it further, and spent some more time on the physical work."

The scene between Crichton and Aeryn in the elevator was largely worked out on the studio floor. "That's the beauty of *Farscape*," David Kemper says. "You have to allow your people to have free rein, and let them make things happen. When we let Ben do it, we have magnificence."

Magnificent is a word also used regularly by cast and crew when referring to the Scarran Emperor, Staleek, who was introduced in this episode. When he realised Duncan Young would be returning later in the season, David Kemper ensured that in his first appearance, in 'I Shrink Therefore I Am', Young's voice was digitised so that he could use his own voice for Staleek. "I think Staleek is Dave Elsey's crowning achievement," Andrew Prowse says. "It was scary just talking to him! All the Scarrans were fabulous — we really got them right."

"This episode had a very specific function in the story arc of this trilogy," Karl Zwicky points out, "and I was determined not to let it become an expositional set-up episode. There are major developments in terms of Scorpius being a spy for the Scarrans! That's a huge revelation in terms of the whole series: he's been a spy for ten arns!"

"At the end of 'Hot to Katratzi', Scorpius looks for all the world as if he really does work for the Scarrans," David Kemper explains. "That reinvigorates the character. People were getting too complacent with him. He was on the ship; he was our friend. Nope — Scorpius is working for himself, folks! We wanted *everything* stacked up against Crichton." ■

Opposite page: Minister Ahkna tortures Scorpius.

Above: Crichton lays down his terms to the Scarrans.

WE'RE SO SCREWED
PART III: "LA BOMBA"

Written by: Mark Saraceni	Guest cast: Paul Goddard (Stark), Rebecca Riggs
Directed by: Rowan Woods	(Grayza), David Franklin (Braca), Duncan Young
	(Staleek), Francesca Buller (Ahkna), Jason Clarke (Jenek)

taleek places Crichton, Scorpius and the rest of Moya's crew under "protective" guard, while Jenek neutralises the systems on board Lo'La. D'Argo and Chiana go back to the ship to try to combat the damage, leaving Scorpius alone with Crichton. The hybrid reveals he is only pretending to be a Scarran spy. His real agenda remains the destruction of the Scarrans. Unfortunately, lacking the wormhole technology that Crichton has successfully resisted sharing with anyone, Scorpius has had to formulate a different plan to halt the Scarran invasion. It seems that a plant known as Crystherium utilia promotes Scarran brain development — and is essential to the existence of the Scarran Ruling Caste. However, Crystherium utilia requires very specific conditions under which to grow; the Scarran base at Katratzi is the only known source in this sector of the galaxy. The destruction of the Crystherium caverns on Katratzi would put a halt to Scarran advancement for many cycles...

Crichton to Chiana

"I can't believe that I left a nuclear bomb in an elevator."

"Well it's alright. You've done worse."

"The whole idea of the flowers came from Wayne Pygram," Andrew Prowse reveals. "To his eternal credit, Wayne spent a lot of season four as Scorpius's 'keeper', making sure the character remained unique, removed and dangerous. He told David that he'd had an image of Scorpius in a field of flowers. It all related back to the end of 'Incubator', where he stroked the flower. The episode was geared around this image of Scorpius in a field of burning flowers."

"David ran with that image," Tim Ferrier adds, "and came up with the whole concept that these flowers were what the Scarrans relied upon. We started having the Scarrans eating the plants much earlier on, but making no conversational reference to it until this episode." "Suddenly we had this huge twist," Prowse continues, "where Scorpius's agenda isn't really wormholes at all, but getting revenge on the Scarrans, using these flowers."

But being *Farscape*, that twist was quickly followed by another. "Scorpius has manipulated Crichton to get him into the position he wants, but then finds he has miscalculated," David Kemper says. "It was one of the first mistakes he's ever made — and the dumb human who he's manipulated has to rescue him!"

"There were exciting aspects to the script," Rowan Woods says, "but what was difficult was the elevator gag. You cannot take that premise too seriously, so we decided to force the *Dr Strangelove* references on it, and mined the potential for absurd comedy and self-deprecation."

"Part of the joy of *Farscape* is that we write it seriously," David Kemper notes, "but everyone understands when it's a comedy and you can get humour out of it." Browder is glad that "for the first time since the Crichton on Talyn died, Claudia and I were able to play. We had a constant by-play." "There was an interesting moment with Ahkna," Claudia Black adds, "where she makes an advance towards Crichton, and Aeryn intercepts. Ahkna walks out, and Ben improvised something about 'She scares me', and I replied, 'I think it's the hat.'"

Although 'La Bomba' was bringing a number of matters to a head, as Crichton detonates the nuclear bomb and destroys the matriarch plant, it was also setting the scene for the next episode, and the fifth year. "Crichton had to do something that *really* annoys the Scarrans," Kemper says, "and by blowing up his base, you're pretty much assured Staleek is going to be pissed off! At the same time, Grayza has miscalculated Crichton and the Scarrans completely. She goes a little bit out of control, so Braca takes over. David

Above: Crichton and Aeryn look down on the flower chamber.

Next page: Crichton demands answers from Scorpius.

Franklin has brought so much to Braca over the years, and I wanted to reward that with great material."

Director and actors alike relished the 'NYPD Blue' scene in the first act, where Crichton is having a conversation simultaneously with Scorpius and Harvey. "We were almost into associative film making," Ben Browder comments, while Woods calls it "esoteric. In many ways it's one of the more intense end points to the story of Scorpius in Crichton's head," Woods adds. "By the end, we have seven minutes of exposition given to you by two guys in two different realities. I think Harvey is one of the best ideas to come out of the show — it's freewheeling storytelling at its best."

"We were heading much more in that disjointed direction," Andrew Prowse says. "I love it when the editing is not dictated by naturalistic events, but by the emotional drive of the story, and the order in which you need to know the information." Prowse credits first assistant director Michael 'Bubba' Feranda and producer Lil Taylor for ensuring that everything came together in the chaotic days at the end of the year. "At this stage of every season, Bubba comes in and juggles all the pieces," Prowse explains. "His schedules are a work of art! Lil worked out what we needed in the scripts, and Bubba dealt with the logistics. They were amazing." ■

☰ BAD TIMING

Written by: David Kemper	Guest cast: Paul Goddard (Stark), David Franklin
Directed by: Andrew Prowse	(Braca), Duncan Young (Staleek), Francesca Buller (Ahkna), John Adam (Pennoch)

aptain Braca informs the crew of Moya that he has intercepted a transmission from Katratzi, indicating that the Scarrans are heading for Earth, the source of a fresh supply of the vital flowers. Leaving Scorpius and Sikozu drifting in space for Braca to collect, Moya StarBursts away. While the Leviathan puts herself at risk by undertaking an extended StarBurst to beat the Scarrans to the mouth of the wormhole leading to Earth, Crichton feverishly studies his equations to find a way to collapse that route to his home planet. But when he finally solves the problem, he realises his primitive human abilities prevent him from piloting his module accurately enough. Only Pilot, with his innate abilities to multitask, could fly a ship into the wormhole at just the right millisecond to cause it to collapse behind them. But Pilot and Moya are unwilling to undergo the risks that the necessary separation of their systems would require…

Crichton to Aeryn

"What did you imagine for your life?"

"Service, promotion, retirement, death. You?"

"This is exactly what I imagined. And a couple of kids."

"What I wanted to do at the end of the year," David Kemper explains, "was show two people who are destined to be together. They love each other completely, and they have said, essentially, 'This is it' — you can almost imagine them quitting the superhero game. Then they're sandbagged by an alien who shoots them right at the moment of their greatest happiness! It's kind of like *Farscape*: Right when you feel you've got it under control, somebody shows up and screws you."

Although no changes were made to the script during the shooting of the episode to reflect the cancellation of the series, a few additions were made in post-production. The episode fades up to what the post-production script describes as "a high-speed kick ass retrospective of four fabulous *Farscape* series", taking two four-frame grabs from each of the preceding eighty-seven

ENCOUNTERS: QUJAGANS

A race whose bodies can adapt to situations, providing special pairs of eyes or other organs whenever they are needed. Their technology has the ability to crystallise carbon-based life forms to enable easy analysis.

episodes before Ben Browder announces, 'And finally on *Farscape*'. The lack of music at the end was also a deliberate choice, to mark the show's passing.

But otherwise, it was business as usual, wrapping up some plotlines and setting others in motion. "This is the way we've always done the show," Kemper says. "The two- or three-parter at the end is the big action/adventure pay off, and the final episode is the first episode of the next season. It's always about emotion, not action, at this stage."

"The cold open is one of David's most interesting bits of writing," Andrew Prowse comments. "You're not sure what the reality is until right at the end. You realise that the time frame is when they're throwing Scorpius off the ship, and everything else happened some time earlier."

Kemper tied himself down to certain scenes very early in the year. "While I was writing 'Unrealized Reality'," he recalls, "I had to write the scene for Jack and John in 'Bad Timing'. I had to lock myself into the end of the year, because we had to film it while [the US-based] Kent McCord was in Australia. He was phenomenal. We spent half a season building up to that scene! The theme of this year is that Crichton realises he can't go home again. He's been in the city too long; he can't go back to the farm. All of his dreams of Earth are antiquated — it's time to come up with new dreams. Their conversation was the heart and soul of this episode."

'Bad Timing' ties together a lot of threads from earlier in the year. "Crichton works out the wormhole equations," Kemper explains, "Chiana's fears of going blind from the first episode were realised. She takes it upon herself to solve things because Stark is a raving lunatic, and she goes blind. There are consequences in the *Farscape* universe."

Andrew Prowse likes the scenes between Scorpius and Sikozu on board the Command Carrier. "I think their little sex scene is very kinky," he notes. "Braca wasn't in that scene in the script, but I happened to be looking up in the window, and there was a fabulous reflection. I told David to go and stand there, and it really looked good!"

Ben Browder was the last actor to finish recording his ADR on the series, and ended up contributing some extra lines, playing the pilot who fires at Crichton and Aeryn in the final scene. "Michael Feranda, who has been feeding lines to the actors for three years, played the guy he's talking to," Deb Peart recalls, "and we figured it was poignant that Ben should provide the voice of the guy who shoots Crichton." "I'd been preaching for a random drive-by alien shooting for some time," Browder adds wryly. "But I didn't realise it would be me!"

"We knew at the beginning of the year the places we were going to, and we got there," David Kemper concludes. "There's so much symmetry to this season, and so much closure." ∎

Opposite page:
Harvey drags Crichton into his Easter Bunny reality.

Above: A happy ending? Crichton asks Aeryn to marry him.

SCRIPT TO SCREEN

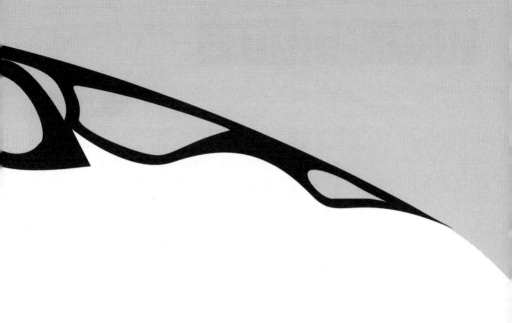

" Your quest is for the princess fair to seek,

the one a human's fleeting love did rend.

Bring forth the sword and through the darkness peek,

One loving kiss amends and there's an end."

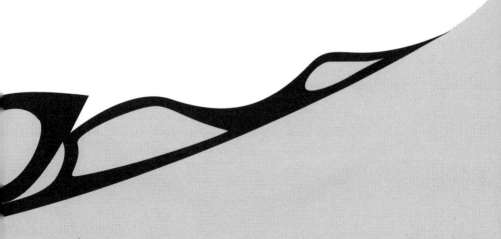

Tony Tilse

"The best part about *Farscape* is that you are able to push things and experiment. 'John Quixote' was a chance to experiment visually. Everyone was always trying to push the boundary a bit further..."

t the end of season two, Crichton and company had started to get a reputation," says Ben Browder. "The question was, what sort of reputation? Everywhere they go, there's death and mayhem. Whether we see them as good guys or bad guys is beside the point. I realised that the vast bulk of the population of the Uncharted Territories must regard our people as terrorists. The Peacekeepers would certainly see them as criminals. That started me thinking about the kinds of stories that would be passing around about 'Crichton and gang'."

David Kemper recalls that 'John Quixote' went through many variations before Ben Browder came up with the idea of the video game. "We worked on this for about five months before we got to something we liked," he says. "One of our ideas was opening in a prison compound, where villagers have been 'resettled' in the way the Nazis did. A father is telling his son a story about Crichton the human and his terrible band of marauders, to distract him from the fact they are going to the gas chambers. Then Crichton appears, and picks up the story, adjusting it. He says, 'I heard Crichton wasn't so bad — I heard he did things to help people, but that's for you guys to decide'.

"During the rest of the episode," Kemper continues, "you realise something is going on, as we see Crichton glancing around to spot D'Argo in the rafters of the room whittling away, Aeryn in the corner spooling some yarn, and Rygel over by the food pot. Then the Nazi-aliens come in and everyone starts screaming. Crichton and Aeryn spring their plan, and destroy the bad guys, freeing all the good people. At the end, Crichton points to the boy and says, 'Tell them John Crichton was here.'"

As Browder continued to develop the story, he became determined to use a fairytale format within the *Farscape* structure. He realised that if he was going to have identifiable fairytale motifs, he would have to use some of Crichton's background and his memories. The only person who had access to those was Stark, at the end of 'Infinite Possibilities' when he communed with the dying Crichton on Talyn. "I wanted the point of view of the fairytale and our people to be an outside point of view," he notes. "That became Stark's interpretation melded with an unknown alien, who's identified as Yoti."

Once Browder came up with the concept of the video game, he spent time with David Kemper and the other writers. His story had to fit into the

ongoing structure of the first part of the fourth season. "When I wrote 'Green Eyed Monster', I had one edict, which was to put Crichton and Aeryn together," he says. "This time the edict was to definitively pull them apart, and this time the emphasis had to come from Crichton. It had to be him saying no to Aeryn."

So what could make Crichton do that? "'John Quixote' plays on Crichton's fears with regard to Aeryn," Browder explains. "And it shows him he is distracted from his other goals because of his focus on Aeryn. He assumes the Princess that Stark refers to is Aeryn, because she is the centre of his universe. But she is a dangerous distraction. During the story, we see he is vulnerable because of her, and will make mistakes because of her. Those mistakes will not only cost other people's lives, but also Aeryn's. It leads him to the point of taking the Laka distillate." Along the way, Browder took the opportunity to present "how our people are perceived — with distortion. Zhaan is a big, fat, ugly man. Rygel is a flatulent flame thrower!"

As he had when he was writing 'Green Eyed Monster', Browder conferred with the people who would be directly involved with his script. "Ben came and talked to me about everything," production designer Tim Ferrier recalls. "Then he went and talked with Terry Ryan about the costumes, prior to delivering the script. He'd tell me his ideas, and I'd tell him what we could do."

Ferrier suggested that visually, the game could be reminiscent of Playstation games that Crichton had played as a youngster. "I looked at early

games like *Spyro The Dragon*," he says. "Platform games with obviously arti-ficial spires and walls. *Spyro* had some almost cartoony graphics in it. It was a 'medieval' game, with castles, pristine green lawns and flowers."

Browder's script required a number of actors to return to the show. "I tried to give folks something that they wanted to do," he explains. "I think it's really important in the creative process to have all the elements as fully engaged as you can get them."

"I loved being back there," Tammy MacIntosh says. "It was all about going home and playing with the kids again. I spent two days on it, and was shooting the other series I'm in, *All Saints*, at the same time. My head was full of two scripts — on one I was in a medical show being a doctor, and on the other, I was being eaten alive with baked beans as my intestines! I decided I wasn't going to analyse my life at that moment! Anthony Simcoe was doing classic kooky Anth — somebody just let him off his leash and let him run." Gigi Edgley enjoyed her scenes with Simcoe and MacIntosh. "We had a lot of fun dangling in D'Argo's dungeon. We had to shoot that scene over many times from different characters' perceptions."

Two actors were required to play Zhaan, and Browder was pleased when negotiations were completed with Virginia Hey, to allow her to recre-

Page 79: Crichton and Chiana wonder what's going to happen next.

Opposite page: Filming Big Zhaan and his van.

Above: Hansel and Gretel prepare to be eaten.

ate her role in the closing scenes. "I was only in for half a day," Hey recalls, "but I had a wonderful time. When I walked on set, and saw Rowan Woods dressed as me, with my make-up on, I nearly died laughing!"

Woods had been "swapping jokes and ideas" about the script with Browder for some months, and the actor had written the part of Big Zhaan with the director in mind. Woods has theatrical training, and was delighted that Browder was serious about casting him. "It was really difficult," Woods remembers. "I was directing 'I Shrink Therefore I Am' immediately afterwards, but I was determined to go for it. It was a hellish schedule in the end — the day before and after I shot the scenes as Big Zhaan, I was directing. I had to be released early, woken at 3am, dragged out to the Olympic Centre where we were shooting in the car park, and then be made up, which took four hours."

"I've never seen a man milk his breasts on television!" Browder notes. "I knew the minute that Big Zhaan milked her breasts we were going to lose a certain segment of the population. There are enough people who can't stand for a woman to breast-feed her child, who respond like it's a sin, or something gross. But it's the most beautiful, natural thing in the world. What the hell's the matter with these people? Zhaan is the show's mother figure. She heals by being the mother figure, so symbolically, it's completely valid!"

Browder was pleased that Tony Tilse was directing his episode, coming in for what turned out to be his swan-song on the show. "Ben had been keeping me up to date on the broad sketches of what he was trying to do," the director says. "When I came on board, the whole concept of the game and the fairy-tale elements were there, and stayed pretty intact."

One location changed. "We were trying to work out the logistics of dealing with the different levels in the game," producer Andrew Prowse says. "The solution we came up with was the car park." "The original plan was to be in an enchanted forest with doors in trees, very much like Tim Burton's *The Nightmare Before Christmas*," Browder explains. "That whole setting was mythical, but we weren't in a position to build the sets, and we couldn't go on location. We had to stay right on budget with this episode! So we worked out another setting where doors would seem familiar, and Tony came up with the idea of the car park. And from that came the idea of a car chase, and vehicles, which led to Zhaan in a van…"

"Which led to the idea of using the van to run Rygel over," Tony Tilse adds. The costume department created a very intricate piece of armour for the Hynerian knight to wear. "Tony was *determined* to run him over," Rygel handler Mat McCoy recalls. "The armour was so well made that it didn't even leave a mark!"

Central to the episode was the Avatar figure of Stark. "Ben called me up to tell me he was writing me a sonnet," Paul Goddard says. "I wondered how he was going to be able to get that past David Kemper, because I never thought they'd let him do it. He had a bit of a battle on his hands, because they thought it was going to take forever to say, but we did it. Ben made it the key clue, so you couldn't chop it out. I worked really hard to make it clear, and not to gabble it."

Dave Elsey and the Creature Shop created the game blobs from their special prosthetic formula, Hot Flesh. "We made boxes full of them," Elsey recalls. "There were three sorts — some with lots of lighting and electronic effects, others that switched on and flashed a bit, and some background ones, that were just painted resin."

Opposite page: The Wicked Witch, aka D'Argo, gets ready for dinner.

Above: The Ogre.

The Creature Shop also put Lani Tupu into prosthetics for his role as the Ogre. "Originally he had three horns coming out of his head," Elsey explains. "I always liked the Ogre in Terry Gilliam's *Time Bandits*, and I wanted to do something on those lines. We got as far as sculpting the horns, and then Andrew Prowse pointed out that there was going to be a big sword fight, so we had to scale them down! We ended up reusing the horns from the Star Goat in 'What Was Lost'."

Tupu didn't particularly enjoy the experience of prosthetics. "Years back, I originally auditioned for D'Argo — but I'm glad I didn't get the part!" he laughs. "I wouldn't have had the patience Anthony has. During the fight sequence, I got a blinding headache and had to step off set for a while to cool down. But it was a fun episode — they recorded about fifteen minutes of Claudia and I snoring together!"

Much of the input for the sequences with Aeryn as the Princess came directly from Claudia Black. "Ben wanted something that was sinister, but in a comic environment," she recalls. "So what he got was *Who's Afraid of Virginia Woolf?* meets Mike Tyson stuck in Vivien Leigh's body! I told Ben that I had a

slightly absurd twist for the Princess, and when I showed him, he really laughed. I showed Tony, and he loved it, and I think it helped him out of a tough spot in the sword fight. We should have had several days to shoot that, but we didn't, so we chucked the Princess on the bed, and then I improvised. As they were fighting, I threw out a heap of lines. The hardest part was keeping a straight face while Ben was falling apart on the other side of the camera. I've never seen him do that before — and it was a gift to be able to get to him like that. He's pretty silly and goofy when he wants to be, so it was a great day when I got him to the point where he just couldn't hold it together!" Browder remembers it well: "She had a weird, fractured, hybrid accent which worked perfectly in the fractured fairytale. She was nothing short of brilliant!"

The section in which Crichton and Chiana think they've returned to Moya grew in importance during the writing stage. "Ben wanted the storyline to be simpler," David Kemper recalls, "but we layered it up with the stuff on the ship. You have the really gorgeous twist of just when you're thinking they're back home, they're still in the game."

"I thought that would be difficult to sustain," Browder admits, "but I got notes from David and the writing staff saying they wanted that section to be bigger. When you get notes from the executive producer, you take the note! People who didn't know the science fiction cliché were totally sucked in when he's on the ship. We put in some little clues. Where are Noranti and

Sikozu? I had to make sure the internal logic of the episode tracked, and it does. Stark only knows what Crichton has mentioned in the game, and that's one of the things I'm most proud of."

Gigi Edgley recalls "a technique Andrew Prowse taught me: when you're manipulating someone, don't act as if you are. In your eyes, you are trying to get them to pursue the best possible outcome for all concerned. In the scenes with the 'game' Chiana, I played her normally until the last stages when there were some technical hitches in her character because of what she didn't know."

Tony Tilse tried to get a different feel to the visual components for the scenes within the game, using digital video cameras and split screens to emphasise the strangeness. "Tony rang and asked what he needed to do to make sure it was alright technically," post-production supervisor Deb Peart remembers. "We did a lot of different treatments on the footage, and at one point, we depolarised the picture to make it look like *Super Mario Brothers*, with heavy pixelations. But that paled in comparison to the ordinary 35mm footage. We ended up using a very basic treatment."

One idea dropped very late in the process was the use of "little health meters on screen. We had different concepts for those, from the traditional video game health bars, to two hearts, a red one for Crichton and a grey one for Chiana, going up and down depending on how they were doing," Peart explains. "In the end we dropped them, because we didn't think it added to what was going on. When they were on Moya, the little health meter would have come out when Crichton got the game ball out. But there was so much going on, you didn't need to add anything more to it."

Guy Gross "had a really good time scoring this one. It took a long time. We knew at the beginning that we could never score it the way a computer game is scored, because you couldn't sustain the joke for that length of time. There were some great sequences: I scored the swordfight with Aeryn on the bed like a recitative in a Mozart operetta, gently underscoring the dialogue. That was a tip of my hat to my upbringing with the classics. The CGI sequence with Zhaan at the end was sweet — we had a full choral section, and I made it as magical as I possibly could."

Browder feels that the original edit of 'John Quixote', which lasts around fifty minutes, "makes much more sense. It's better, because there's time to think about what is occurring. Often it works well for *Farscape* to compress, but this is a little too compressed. But that's because there are one or two too many people in the story. But I don't know what pieces I could do without."

Overall, however, 'John Quixote' achieves what it sets out to do. "It's the set up for the drive through the year," Browder concludes. "There's always two edges to *Farscape*: seriousness hidden in comedy, and comedy hidden in seriousness. To the casual eye, it might seem flippant. To me, it's anything but!" ■

Opposite page:
Harvey and The
Princess wait for their
gentleman caller.

THE CHARACTERS

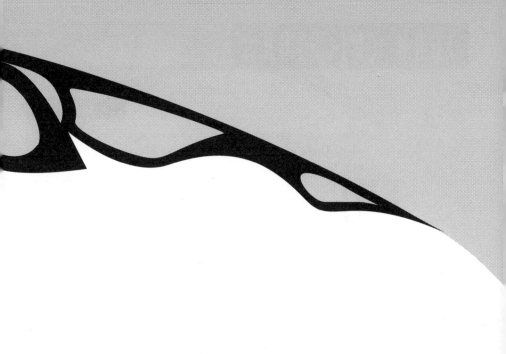

" You might not want to come with us. We are not the best

travelling companions."

– John Crichton

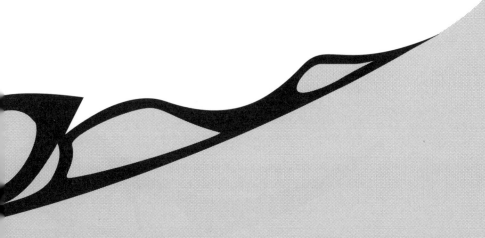

Crichton

" I'm not fast enough. I am not alien enough. And you know what? There are people in the universe who don't like me. I'm only human."

n the original tag for the première episode," Ben Browder recalls, "Rockne O'Bannon had a line where Crichton's recording the tape for his father and he says, 'And there's this girl...' The tag changed to accommodate certain things, but I always took that as Rockne's intent, and took it as a truism for the series. Crichton and Aeryn's relationship is the heart of the series. The heart of *The Odyssey* is a love story about a man trying to get home to his wife. In *Farscape*, Aeryn becomes home for Crichton."

Crichton begins the fourth season separated not just from Aeryn, but from everyone that he has come to know during his time in the Uncharted Territories. On board the dying Leviathan Elack, he is busy working out the wormhole equations and has just about succeeded when the ship is attacked. "I like seeing Crichton this way," Browder says. "This is his reaction to the universe: he's isolated, but he's going to solve the wormholes before he dies. He's clinging to hope — a theme that we constantly return to during the show. I don't know that he's the most accessible character at the start of the year, but he's certainly interesting!"

Browder understands the story reasons for the scenes between Crichton and Grayza in 'What Was Lost', even if he felt uncomfortable during the filming. "When they meet on Katratzi, Crichton is unable to deal with Grayza, because of the way she dealt with him on Arnessk," he agrees. "It's an interesting moment when he turns to her in 'La Bomba' and asks her if she feels 'frelled, screwed, raped'. There are certain people you don't deal with, and I think those earlier scenes set up a barricade between them. Grayza may be being reasonable and honourable on Katratzi, but the truth is, you're talking about someone who rapes to get what she wants."

When he returns to Moya in 'Promises', Crichton finds himself in a totally unforeseen predicament. "I think so many things pivot on that moment when Aeryn makes him promise her he won't hurt Scorpius," Browder reflects. "When Crichton is forced to make a promise, he won't break it. He is a man of his word. That's one of his redeeming and heroic qualities. If he says he's going to do something, he's going to do it, or die trying. At the moment Aeryn makes him promise, he was ready to blast Scorpy out into space."

Browder considers that all of Crichton's behaviour in the middle part of the season, from 'Promises' to the end of 'Twice Shy', stems from that moment. "He has to live with that," he notes. "How does he keep this

promise to Aeryn, and still protect her at the same time? John's greatest fear is that Scorpius is going to use Aeryn. When Aeryn says 'jump', John asks how high? He knows this about himself."

Crichton's solution is one of the three things he does during the year that Browder considers "reprehensible". "That's the reason he starts taking the Laka beetle distillate," he says. "In 'John Quixote' the Zhaan figure asks him how many more people will die for love of him. He has to protect Aeryn, and everyone else around him. He doesn't want the feelings of love to end. When you love someone, no matter how bad it is, you don't want it to end. The pain is better. You take the good with the bad when you're in love, and Crichton is still in love. He can't stop being in love with Aeryn, and since he can't, Aeryn is at risk, and the baby is at risk. Scorpius has told him that a war is coming, and the chess pieces are in play. Crichton is a piece on the board. He doesn't want to be, but he is. Being a piece puts everyone around him in danger constantly, whether it's Aeryn or the baby. It may not be his, but as far as he's concerned, it is."

Crichton feels the same way when, totally unexpectedly, he finds himself back on Earth. "He doesn't fit in there," Browder says. "The other people on Moya fit in more than he does! He believes he shouldn't be there, because he's

putting everybody in danger. He's still thinking about how to protect people from him. The Scarrans are going to come down the wormhole, and Grayza's out there. His thrust throughout 'Terra Firma' is that they've got to leave. Earth isn't ready, and he's not ready. It's where he thought he wanted to be, but he can't think about that now."

When Aeryn finally confronts him at the end of 'Twice Shy', "Crichton doesn't understand what he's done to her. Crichton and Aeryn always have the best intentions for each other, but they never understand that." The period of reconciliation is short-lived, and after Aeryn is kidnapped by the Scarrans, Crichton commits his second reprehensible act. "He allies himself with Scorpius to get Aeryn back, because he perceives he's going to be incapable of doing it on his own," explains Browder. "He makes a deal with the devil — which has its own consequences later on."

During the hunt for Aeryn, Crichton is much more focused. "From the moment she's abducted, there's not a lot of lightness or wisecracking," Browder says. "He can bluster his way through saving the universe, but not through saving Aeryn. He's deadly serious then. It was good to finally get Aeryn back, because it alleviated that." The return of Harvey triggers Crichton's final reprehensible act, going to Katratzi rather heavily armed. "He goes and drops a nuclear bomb! He's made three really hard choices. I like the fact Crichton is supporting capitalism. Does the American want democracy? No. He wants capitalism — but backed by a bomb!" Even with all that going on, Crichton and Aeryn do get to "go to the prom. The scene in the elevator is the defining romantic moment for John and Aeryn," Browder maintains. "We sprung that on the director, Karl Zwicky, and God bless him, he shot it. Crichton and Aeryn finally get a chance to dance, even if in typical *Farscape* fashion, they do it while travelling from point A to B surrounded by danger."

Browder admits he was feeling pessimistic when he and Claudia Black shot John and Aeryn's final scene. "We were getting into the boat, and I said to Claudia, 'This could be the last thing we ever shoot together,'" he recalls. "She said, 'No, there'll be another year'. But it was our last scene." Browder recognises there are still unanswered questions, but concludes, "If we'd done season five and known we were going to end, it would have been interesting to see which plots we did conclude, which threads we did tie up, which questions we did answer. Mind you, I think if the series had gone on for *ten* years, you wouldn't have got all the answers!" ■

Aeryn

" I did everything, everything I could to keep us together. I did exactly what you told me to do, and the whole time, you have been cheating."

"I never had a problem playing someone who was desperately flawed, sometimes unlikeable, inappropriate and violent," says Claudia Black. "What always appealed to me was that Aeryn has the potential to grow, and by the end of the series, she has fallen completely and utterly in love with a man who's so separate from her experience of life. The less afraid she became, and the more she opened herself up and yielded to what she couldn't control, the more appealing she became."

Although we see a brief glimpse of a heavily pregnant Aeryn Sun in 'Crichton Kicks', the former Peacekeeper's first proper fourth season appearance is in 'Promises'. "Each year it's been harder to keep Crichton and Aeryn away from each other," Black notes, "or to justify keeping them apart. We wanted them to have a proper break, so that we weren't cheating the audience out of a realistic separation."

This fitted with David Kemper's plan to reintroduce the characters gradually across the first few weeks of the season. "We needed to establish some kind of visual marker for the time that had passed," Black adds, "hence the hair extensions. I wanted some kind of punk hairstyle that would show Aeryn had really been through something, to keep it mysterious. I felt my job in season four was to maintain as much mystery about what Aeryn had been up to as possible, so that we'd have lots of room to play again. I wanted her to have a new type of pain, a new set of experiences. We may not have had the opportunity to reveal them, but at least it gave her a new foundation."

When she returns to Moya, Aeryn is unaware Crichton knows she's pregnant. "I think she's just expecting that because they've connected again, things will be fine," Black says. "I think that's part of the child in Aeryn: she expects things to happen without a lot of talk. But she should know Crichton better. At the end of 'Natural Election', she realises it's going to be harder than she hoped."

As the season progressed, Black found herself contributing to Aeryn's development. "I came up with the concept of her having a little sitting point. She wants to catch Crichton at the crossroads no matter which way he's going," she explains. "Moya was her home, but she couldn't be home without Crichton. If they're not sharing a bedroom, she'd rather be out of her room, roaming around the ship trying to keep tabs on him."

Black also encouraged the relationship between Aeryn and Sikozu. "There's so much antagonism between everyone on Moya all the time," she

notes. "If people are constantly bickering or being violent and negative, it becomes gratuitous — like slamming each other against a bulkhead to resolve arguments, rather than talking about them. We wanted that relationship to be founded on mutual respect."

This was particularly relevant in 'Bringing Home the Beacon'. "I wanted to make sure that Aeryn didn't make all the decisions," Black says. "I wanted her to be constantly offering Sikozu the opportunity to dip out, but at the same time, Aeryn was very clear she had something that she wanted to do. We ended up making it a sort of *Butch Cassidy and the Sundance Kid* for the girls: Sikozu has opportunities to do something she wouldn't ordinarily do, and she steps up to the plate."

At the end of that episode, Aeryn is captured, but by this stage she and Crichton have come to an understanding, following their visit to Earth and the tag scene at the end of 'Twice Shy'. "I really wanted them to expand on Aeryn's isolation when she was on Earth in 'Terra Firma'," Black recalls. "I wanted more of Crichton's sister in the episode. I thought the audience would be interested in the rest of Crichton's family, not just Jack, and the best way to expose Crichton and Aeryn's experiences was through the sister. I also asked Ricky Manning for a scene between Aeryn and Caroline where they're not actually fighting over the man that they love. They're having an intelligent conversation, acknowledging how awkward life can be, and trying to deal with it in a mature fashion. That's exactly what Ricky gave me."

At the end of 'Twice Shy', "it was very important that Aeryn was so furious with Crichton for taking the drugs. How dare he tell her to get her story straight when the whole time he's been cheating? We needed to hear she was frustrated with this human game: he'd established the rules, and then cheated. How could they communicate as two people if he did that? She's confused by the game. She's always that underdeveloped child who says, 'That's not fair!'"

When Crichton rescues Aeryn from the Scarrans' claws, "I really wanted to push into an area of awkwardness," Black says. "It's the only time we will ever really see her completely stripped down and blubbering. She's a damaged creature trying to shield herself from the light."

Black notes that Aeryn becomes little more than Crichton's 'muscle' during the raid on Katratzi, but there were still opportunities for them to show their love. The scene in the elevator as they go down to the flower room in 'Hot to Katratzi' was a late addition to the script. "I thought I should stand on Crichton's toes and not know how to dance," Black comments. "I always like reminding the audience that Aeryn is inexperienced. It's a nice moment for them, with some romance and tenderness."

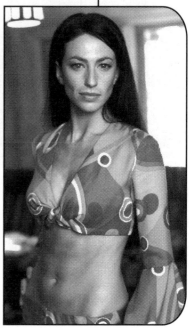

Initially Aeryn was going to be yet another hindrance to Crichton as he made his plan to save Earth in 'Bad Timing'. "I had to speak up about that," Black says. "If we were going to play this as a romantic tale, then the woman who has pride of place next to the man in her life would understand what he needs, and when he needs time alone. We needed to see these people operating together, bringing out the best in each other. I wanted it to be obvious that they're operating with such seamless shorthand. She's his muse, the source of his inspiration. And she has total confidence in him. If she can't have faith in him, no one can."

The final scene in the boat continues the concept of inexorability that Black and Browder tried to bring to the lovers' relationship. "If two people are meant to be together, nothing will tear them apart. In that last sequence, when they're crystals, they're intermingled more than they could be any other way. It's just one more thing that's an impediment to their love. The essence of their characters was that they fought. He learned to become a warrior and a hero. Aeryn has always been at her best in battle. The end, where they go out in such a heroic and romantic way, combines the two elements beautifully. 'There's nothing we can do — let's go out on a kiss.' I think that's a pretty cool way to go. Especially if you're kissing Ben Browder!" ■

"I am violent when I choose to be. And right now, I choose not to kill you. But that could change."

or me, the challenge is always creating subtle change," Anthony Simcoe explains. "If I rest back on my laurels, it becomes boring for everyone. And when boredom sets in, then you start to do really bad work. My anchor points for creating that change in season four were how D'Argo was going to deal with the challenges of captaining the ship, and the rebuilding of the relationship with Chiana."

Simcoe has always wanted to ensure that "if you put on episode ten of season three and then episode ten of season four, you wouldn't see the same person", and in addition to the changes that he brought to the part through his performance, there were physical differences between the third and fourth years. "I got a new make-up team in season four," he recalls, "and they were the fastest ever. They didn't change the design — in the two previous seasons, we had done a great job of streamlining it as much as we could. But I did have a costume change midway through the year. I didn't really like my costume much at the start of the season, but it was built for comfort. It was the lightest costume I ever wore, but I think it was the least effective both aesthetically and visually. The final costume I wear on *Farscape* is a combination of my season one coat and my season two and three outfits, with bits from both. I absolutely *loved* that costume — I was happy to finish the season wearing that, because I think D'Argo just looked really cool!"

Like all the crew of Moya, D'Argo had various adventures when he was away from the ship between the seasons, but unlike some of the others' experiences, D'Argo's were positive. "He came back strong, and had actually had a great time," Simcoe explains. "Aeryn and Chiana came back after really traumatic experiences, but D'Argo came back after the break a little more comfortable in his skin. That leads to him being captain. If he had been too battered around, then he wouldn't have been able to take up the mantle of protecting the other people on the ship. I think that's how D'Argo feels now — he has discovered that his future and his family really revolve around these people."

Not everyone was happy with D'Argo's promotion to captain. In 'A Prefect Murder', even Crichton has to be put in his place. "It set a bit of barrier between D'Argo and the other characters," Simcoe agrees. "That was interesting to play, but it eventually starts to settle down, and everyone begins to accept their role within the family. I liked that when he became captain, he didn't suddenly become this all-knowing character.

But there were certainly moments throughout the season where suddenly he's being deferred to by the others, when he never would have been before. Confronting those challenges, and either succeeding or bailing, added a lovely dimension for me to play."

Simcoe was glad the writers made D'Argo a flawed leader. "Not that I thought he was a terrible captain," he adds swiftly, "but he wasn't Jean-Luc Picard! He was someone struggling through new responsibility. But I think he grew into it. He grew two inches taller when he became captain. You got the sense that he was going to become a really successful leader. He deals with everything — leading, comforting people, guidance and the high stake decision making — and in general succeeds at a lot of them."

The brief relationship with Jool in 'What Was Lost' surprised Simcoe to an extent. "That was a bit out of the blue," he notes. "I don't think it arced through strongly enough to deserve the weighted moment it had at the end." However, he was delighted by the handling of the rekindling of D'Argo's relationship with Chiana. "That relationship brings out more complexity in both of them, regardless of whether they make a good couple or not," he maintains. "They generate some great drama when they're together, and interacting at a more complex level. It was great to be able to dive back into that relationship. Gigi and I were never happy about the

way we broke up, because it was so abrupt. There wasn't an organic arc out of it, but this season, there was an organic arc back into it. It happened slowly and steadily, with small bits of information introduced from episode to episode."

D'Argo also faced one of his demons, facing down and finally defeating his wife's murderer, Macton, in 'Mental as Anything'. "It was great to explore that backstory finally," Simcoe says. "We wanted to toughen D'Argo up again, and let the mantle of his responsibility on the ship sit well on his shoulders. What I like most about *Farscape* is that they're imperfect characters. They aren't superheroes. They're full of tension. They've got hatred and anger, and dark and evil things inside them. It would be so boring if the characters were all pure and clean, and everything they did was good!"

Working on the episode exhausted Simcoe. "There was just so much raw emotional content," he explains. "Every episode of *Farscape* deals with emo-

tions, but only rarely do they come up quite as raw as that." Simcoe feels it was well worth the effort. "It fed into D'Argo's comprehension of himself as captain," he says. "Once you face those big, soul-searching questions, you come out a stronger character at the end. His reaction to Macton now is very different from what it would have been earlier in the series — but it's still a very just punishment. D'Argo gets his revenge, but comes out a bit wiser."

Simcoe enjoyed the group dynamic of the majority of the season. "Storylines had become so separated over the last couple of years," he points out. "Even when we were on the ship, there were so many different, strong threads. This year, it was like season one, where we had five characters in a room solving problems. I think we had some really beautiful group scenes. In other seasons you'd notice the moments between individual characters, but this year, the highlight was when all the characters were on set together. It was a warm way to finish the show."

Like the rest of the cast, Simcoe was devastated by the cancellation, and would return to the part if called. "D'Argo is the most fun character I have ever played in my life," he says bluntly. "He fits firmly and squarely into what I love most about acting — trying to become something that is so completely removed from me as a person. I want to become unrecognisable, and D'Argo is the absolute personification of that ideal. To play him was the gift of a lifetime." ∎

" It's just the dark. You don't know what's coming and there's nothing you can do. I hate that feeling."

"Season four tested me physically, emotionally, mentally and spiritually," Gigi Edgley admits. There was a conscious effort by all departments to recreate the unstable alien who first came on board Moya in season one. "We spent a lot of time in the chair trying to bring her make-up back to her old self," Edgley recalls, and producer Andrew Prowse adds, "She'd become a bit too manicured at the end of season three, so we tried to make her look a bit woollier and out of control. We wanted to bring back that edge of unpredictability about her, make her more wild and dangerous."

At the start of the year, Chiana is definitely out of control, lashing out physically and verbally. "'Crichton Kicks' birthed some beautifully depicted emotions as a consequence of what happened to her during the time the crew spent apart," Edgley notes. "David Kemper and Brian Henson both wanted to see a more dangerous side of this little lost alien. David gave me a brief description of what had occurred between the seasons — she was forced to face some of her greatest fears, which meant that a slightly altered Chiana returned to Moya."

Chiana was raped and possibly tortured, and Edgley acknowledges that "Chiana invited me to play with her more animalistic characteristics, which had helped her survive in the wild unknown. Her heart was broken and strewn across the galaxy in more ways than one."

The early part of the year gave Edgley other opportunities to demonstrate "the murky waters Chiana dappled in whilst the worlds continued to turn." In 'Natural Election', she has to once again face her fears, which Edgley thinks "she hides from to this day. When she's in the roof of Moya after having a taste of the plant's foreboding nature, I think it brought back to her being stranded deep in the Uncharted Territories, and the nightmares she faced during that time. I cherish scenes like that, because they colour in the parts of Chiana's journey the audience hasn't seen."

During her time away from the ship, Chiana's powers modified. She was now able effectively to slow down time so she can observe everything in incredible detail. But this gift comes at a price. Each time she uses it, her sight takes longer to return, and at the end of 'Bad Timing', she is totally reliant on D'Argo to tell her what is happening between Crichton and Aeryn.

. "'Bad Timing' was a huge learning experience," Edgley says. "As an actor, I wish I had known about the cancellation of the series when I was shooting those scenes. I really wanted to keep the honesty of Chi's fear

when she loses her vision, to really feel how lost one is when all that you know, all that you are, is swept away from you."

Edgley describes the visions as "another challenge in Chiana's world. Each day on and off the set I explored what it would be like to have the blessing of the visions, and how fearful the aftermath would be. It is phenomenal how your other senses react when sight is no longer available. I would sit in my trailer and at home for hours at a time, attempting to function with my eyes closed. Every sound causes your heart to flutter, and you become extremely aware of how lonely this world can be. It made me wonder what blind people dream about."

To achieve the blind look, Edgley initially had to wear full sceleral lenses, covering her entire eyeball. "That was an intense process," she says. "It was made worse if we were shooting blind sequences with those lenses, and then the ordinary black lenses I wear as Chiana on the same day, which at times was quite common.

"It always proved challenging to do the line run-throughs and the blocking of the action without vision," she adds. "You realise the eyes really *are* the windows to one's soul! It's hard to communicate with people when you can't tell where the voices are coming from. It was amazing how differently people would treat you on the set. I think at times it was frustrating for the other actors, directors and crew working with a vision-

impaired actor. But it really helped my craft taking it all in, and using it for those scenes."

As the season progressed, "we shipped in a smaller pair of lenses which only covered the iris. Before then, there were just pinpricks in the lenses for eyeholes, so you might be able to see shapes, depending on the light. It taught me to surrender to the moment. With the new lenses, the vision was still pretty restricted, but the pain factor was non-existent, thank goodness."

Edgley was pleased to see the relationship with D'Argo reawaken, starting with the Chinese whispers sequence in 'Natural Election'. "That started to build a stronger bond between them," she notes. By the time they reached Earth in 'Terra Firma', "the writers were pushing the D'Argo and Chiana relationship again, but they weren't quite sure what to do with it, so Anthony and I tried to leave it as open as possible."

The actress also enjoyed the relationships Chiana forged with the other girls on board. "It's awesome when the girls get to play together," she laughs. "We can find out who they are, and what they are all about. Raelee and I had fun conjuring up how to fly D'Argo's ship in 'Lava…' Aeryn and Chiana formed a beautifully delicate friendship — a combination of teacher, mother, sister and friend. And when we were on the commerce station in 'Bringing Home the Beacon', I think Chi realised that Noranti was a crazy alien who'd be a good playmate."

Edgley thinks "it's sometimes easy to lose detail when one is focusing on the bigger picture. One of the most beautiful things about *Farscape* was that we would go to the ends of the universe to tell the most impactful story for the audience, even if did mean sacrificing the honesty of individual character arcs." She feels the final few episodes might have gone down that road, but "it's not necessarily a disadvantage if you can make it work for you. It's just tricky sometimes figuring out how." Her final scene shot for the series was for 'A Constellation of Doubt', where Chiana is in the bathroom asking Bobby about humanity's use of water. "I decided I needed to fit everything I always wanted to do with Chiana into it," she recalls. "I felt completely taken away with the words Chiana was saying. All of a sudden they had a very different meaning."

Edgley will always value the *Farscape* experience. "I learned to surrender to the moment, trust my instincts and always embrace each opportunity," she says. The young Nebari she played evidently took on a life of her own over the years. "She has shown me some wonderful worlds in places once unseen," Edgley concludes. "Chiana has taught me about the courage that stirs in one's belly to make you set out, and go on an adventure!" ■

" We are natural allies, John. The Scarrans will ravage your planet, and I can prevent it."

uring *Farscape*'s fourth year, viewers saw a very different side of Scorpius, as the Scarran-Sebacean half-breed became a fixture on board Moya — albeit one who wasn't trusted by most of his shipmates. Stripped of his position in the Peacekeeper hierarchy following the destruction of his Command Carrier at the end of the third season, Scorpius was apparently betrayed by his formerly loyal second in command, Braca. When we meet Scorpius on Grayza's Carrier, he seems to have lost everything.

"He gave it all away," Wayne Pygram explains. "He put himself in a position where he was vulnerable." Pygram suggested that Scorpius should be walking around on all fours. "No one expected that!" he recalls. "I didn't even think about it until they put the dog collar on. We rehearsed the scene with me being led around, and I thought we should try it differently. Thankfully we had Rowan Woods directing, who loved it."

Although Pygram's creative juices were flowing at the start of the year, he himself was suffering internally. "I wasn't well. The lining of my intestine was breaking down," he explains. "The start of the season was horrible for me because I was so sick. I was worried I had cancer. I was losing weight, and my suit was getting really skinny. You can see it flapping off me; everyone thought I was so good to lose weight for the scenes. They thought I was that committed to playing Scorpius's frailty! But I was really suffering. I was in deep trouble, and it was hard to share that with the team at work. We had new people, and I wanted to make them feel welcome, and be there for them. But I was coming home and laying down on the couch. The next thing I know, it's 3am, I haven't moved, and I've got to go to work two hours later. I couldn't cook, or even go out and get a takeaway." Eventually, Pygram was diagnosed with a condition that required him to eliminate all the gluten from his diet, and thankfully he started to recover.

By this stage, Scorpius had come on board Moya. "We discussed the idea at the end of the third year, and I knew when I started this season that I would be on the ship by episode five," he recalls. "They didn't know what they were going to do with him, just that it would be delicate having him there. But it created as many problems as it solved by bringing him on board. The main problem we had then was replacing the best villain in science fiction!" Pygram isn't convinced that it was ultimately the right move for the character. "I think it was a bit of a stitch-up in the end," he admits. "It meant that for me, it was a year of treading water."

Pygram initially wasn't certain himself why Scorpius was there. "It was partly to do with the wormholes, of course," he says. "He's got to convince Crichton to do the numbers, and the best place to do that is to be nearby, so he can watch him, and control him in some way. That was the only thing I could really latch onto. I had to remind myself that he had another agenda, even if I didn't know what it was! I think personally that Scorpius was driven by his own fever for knowledge."

By the middle of the year, Scorpius's agenda was becoming clearer, and Pygram was given different challenges with his portrayal. "The second half of the season was more satisfying for me, because he actually got to go somewhere," he explains. "When they're on Katratzi, his passion starts overriding his common sense and his intelligence. He's losing, and he's out of control. That's a rare place to see Scorpius. But it's not a bad place dramatically, because there's only one person who can make him stop — and that's John Crichton. It's interesting that the only person who can actually get through to him is Crichton."

At other times, Sikozu is also able to breach some of Scorpius's barriers. From their first meeting, where he saves her life by passing on a mysterious piece of Peacekeeper Security Directorate code, to their last scene as lovers on the deck of Braca's Command Carrier, there is a definite chemistry between them. "That came out of the work during the year," Pygram notes. "It seemed like it was setting something up for later."

Sikozu gives Scorpius what Pygram believes is the half-breed's first kiss. "He's never been kissed before! There's not a lot left that he hasn't tasted, experienced or touched on in his time, but Sikozu gets him with a kiss. He has occasional moments of child-like innocence and naïvety. There isn't much naïvety in him, but when you do see it, it's interesting. He also has an unbelievable coldness, which we see in that alternate reality when he shoots Chiana. He balances between those two areas. He's brutally cold, yet has an innocence you see in the moment of that kiss, when he's pretty vulnerable."

Pygram was pleased that the neural clone Harvey was resurrected before the season came to a close. "The *Nosferatu* scene at the end of 'Fetal Attraction' and the *NYPD Blue* scene in 'La Bomba' were two of the best Harvey bits I've done," he maintains. "Thank the Lord he did come back, because he was sorely missed — certainly he was missed by the crew, and I think he was by the audience as well. I really missed him too! I had a ball with the sheer variety of it. The Easter Bunny scene was totally silly, indulgent and wonderful. But then again it was the last scene I shot on *Farscape*, so I'll buy it even if it doesn't quite work."

Pygram also enjoyed the opportunity to play Crichton's father in one of the unrealized realities, giving a very accurate take on Kent McCord's performance. "It was transforming to put on a reality-based make-up," he recalls, "and to actually play someone who's in the cast. I immediately said we should do it again, and I think we would have."

Pygram was looking forward to working one-on-one with other actors in the fifth year, rather than in group scenes. "I felt awkward in the big group scenes, because I'm so used to driving everything," he explains. "It felt really odd to be just a part of the fabric of a group scene. I really wanted to go back to how it used to be!"

Pygram doesn't expect to continue his career performing in prosthetics. "I'm not going to become a guy that does the big make-up," he says firmly. "But there is one character I will always do, if it's offered, and that's Scorpius. I would never allow anyone else to play him if I was in a position to choose, and I would put the make-up on tomorrow, or next year, or in ten years' time." ■

"I like that you're always striving to reach higher, hoping for a better tomorrow. It's the quality that first attracted me to your uncle."

hat I love about *Farscape* is that it's a TV show, in which I can act very theatrically if I need to!" Melissa Jaffer says fondly. The veteran Australian actress first appeared on the series as the older Nilaam, and the voice of both the younger and older versions of the Orican priest in the second season episode, 'Vitas Mortis'. By one of those odd coincidences that permeate *Farscape*, Dave Elsey decided to use her head cast for Nilaam when he was creating the preliminary designs for the then-unnamed Old Woman at the end of the third season.

"I loved the experience of working with Dave Elsey and his team on 'Vitas Mortis'," she recalls, "and apparently he'd been saying that he thought they might cast me as Noranti. As Dame Edna Everage would say, that was rather spooky! The producers called me in and asked me to look at the role. I loved it, they wanted me to do it, so there it was."

Jaffer was highly impressed by the character breakdown she was presented with by David Kemper. "David said he wanted to give the series back some soul," she says. "Although a lot of the character didn't evolve in the way I expected it to from the breakdown, perhaps the Divine Eternal will take her to those places in the future. Her mind is open and she is wise, and she's spent 293 cycles going wherever the Divine Eternal took her. Wisdom is never closed to change, and her horizons were limitless. She is a very spiritual being, and is aware of another reality outside the one she can see. She has her noetic third eye, through which she can see things other people can't. She's a true mystic. She's also very intelligent, and by the second half of the season, the writers were giving her some good moments."

The actress didn't want Noranti to just be a "dotty old lady. One of the reasons I took the role was because they weren't writing her as that. It's such an insult at my age to be asked to play nothing but dotty old ladies! Many writers can't write for women who are older. They don't know what to do once you get out of the sexual realm, and are no longer interesting sexually. But you have intelligence. You have wisdom. You have experience. You have expertise. They can write those things for men, but they haven't started writing them for women. Noranti has an element of that coming in, which I liked. I never had a problem with the later scripts, because they always wrote very well for my character. Justin Monjo and Ricky Manning particularly liked her: they liked to get quite verbose and my character could deliver that sort of dialogue. There was a florid character to the actual words they were writing for me. They were a delight to deliver, and they loved writing them!"

'Coup by Clam' made it very clear that Noranti was still a sexual being to a certain extent. "You have to understand that Noranti is a person of the present moment," Jaffer explains. "She has a huge memory bank that is dormant, and when someone presses a button, things come flooding back. So in that scene, she's wondering what's happening to her — and of course, she's an alien, so I don't know what an alien would do in that situation! If she has a button and she uses it, I can't control that."

Utu Pralatong Noranti is the character's full name, "and when she remembers it," Jaffer says, "she states it with great dignity, and she knows that she's a doctor. She doesn't think she's old — she might be 293, but Noranti has no conception of what that means as far as an Earthling like John Crichton is concerned. In her head, she's eighteen years old. But her memory is not always there, and it frustrates her because she can't remember why. She might be in the middle of a recipe, and the ingredients escape her. When she has her moments of lucidity, she can see through to the end of a problem."

As the season progresses, Noranti's fondness for Crichton is shown more regularly. She provides him with the Laka beetle juice to help him forget Aeryn, and can be very cutting to the former Peacekeeper at times, even though she's

aware Aeryn is carrying Crichton's child. She also shows a cold-blooded logic that can put the other characters to shame. "If it comes down to a choice between Crichton dying or millions dying, then, sorry Crichton, you have to go," Jaffer points out. "The ends justify the means to her. And she will use any means — she'll even kill somebody if she thinks the world will benefit from it.

"Noranti has in her all the qualities that Zhaan had," Jaffer notes, "but I never had the chance to display them. One of the problems with replacing the 'soul' that Virginia Hey created with her ethereal look as the blue lady, Zhaan, was that they brought in a grubby, dirty old woman! The packaging was such a statement." Noranti did start to build a strong relationship with Pilot and Moya however, and when the Leviathan looks as if she is dying in 'Natural Election', "Noranti completely drops her bundle. She's overwhelmed with

sadness, because the Leviathan is such a good thing, and good things shouldn't have to die."

Noranti doesn't really bond with Sikozu, possibly suspecting the Kalish's Bioloid nature before the others in the crew learn about it at the end of the season. "Noranti distrusts this robotic way that she approaches life," Jaffer comments. "But she gets on very well with Chiana — she likes her very much. Chiana calls Noranti Wrinkles, and isn't unkind to her."

Jaffer describes *Farscape* as "a runaway train once it starts. We call that the Kemper Factor! It's what keeps it sparky, bright and alive, because you never quite know what David's going to ask you to do next. Often you don't know until the night before. It means you don't have a chance to be lulled into a false sense of complacency, which I like."

The actress was looking forward to the fifth season, and the chance to tap into some of the as yet unrealised potential of her character. "By the time I came into the show, Crichton and Aeryn were locked into this deep relationship, and there wasn't a lot of room for any other character to really develop," she notes. "Noranti should have developed along the lines that the blue lady would have, perhaps. But don't get me wrong: I loved *Farscape*. It was so much fun!"

"You do realise that this is a damaged Leviathan with a fraudulent Pilot and a crew of idiots, do you not? They need help!"

he first time I ever wore my whole costume, with my contact lenses in and my wig on, was about five minutes before I went on set," Raelee Hill recalls. "They were screaming for me, but I said, 'I'm just going to go to the bathroom!' I went into the bathroom, stood in front of the mirror, and took five minutes to just look at myself and go, 'Okay, this is what you've got to work with. Great. Now go out there with a thousand words and try and get something down on tape!'"

Raelee Hill initially auditioned for the part of Grayza (who knows, maybe there's an unrealized reality out there in which she was cast in that role...). "She didn't strike me at all as Grayza, but she just had something about her," David Kemper recalls. "She's one of the most likeable people that you could ever meet in person, and that came through on film. Auditioning for Grayza, she was trying to be a nasty person, and even when she was being particularly nasty — and she's a phenomenal actress — she was likeable. I decided that over the summer, I would create a part for her."

"I was given a very small synopsis when I started," Hill says. "Sikozu was from a race called the Kalish, which was a race new to the show. She's a very intellectually driven character. She's very clever, with a photographic memory. She's more brains than brawn. She can throw a punch, but she's not going to pick up any gun in the universe and know exactly what to do with it She's naïve about life, in that she's never really left her company or her government. She's never been out in the wide-open world before. When we meet her in 'Crichton Kicks', she's on her first assignment."

Hill was also told that Sikozu was a robot of some sort. "I knew that from the first day," she reveals, "but I didn't know I was going to be a Bioloid. I was given a specific direction not to make her robotic at all. That was the big reveal. She was going to be organic and like everybody else. There would be nothing at all robotic about her, so it would come as a big surprise."

The actress actually learned she was playing a Bioloid at the end of the day on which the cast shot the climactic scene in 'Bringing Home The Beacon', when it's revealed Aeryn has been replaced by a Bioloid. "It would have been nice if I had known from the executives earlier that same day, because I could have coloured the scene a little bit more," Hill notes, "but that's the nature of the beast. It's one of the best parts of doing television, because you don't know what's around the corner. Things stay fresh for you."

Introducing her character in *TV Guide*, David Kemper hinted there might be some sexual chemistry between Sikozu and Crichton, but that

didn't happen. "We couldn't service everybody and have Crichton fall in love with another girl," he explains.

Like Jool in the third year, Sikozu found herself mistrusted and on the outside of the core Moya crew. "I'd never done a show where I was the outsider," she comments. "It was very interesting to walk on set and have every single character in the show, including Pilot, regard me as an outsider. I was trying to have these little allegiances with people because that's what the audience want to see. They want to see the strength and the gang spirit, but I was the blacklisted girl! I was constantly written forsaking my crewmates, acting as if I didn't care if they survived, just so long as I did, and it got quite frustrating."

However, the one alliance Sikozu did forge helped to alienate her from the rest of the crew. "I took one look at Wayne and knew that his would be the character I wanted to play with the most," Hill says. "I love Scorpius. I think he is *gorgeous*. What's not to love about Scorpy? Look at him. He just wants a big cuddle!"

The chemistry is there from her very first scene with Pygram in 'What Was Lost'. "He confides some information to her and she then jumps out of the grave to talk to Grayza and try to save him," she recalls. "A tiny little alle-

giance starts all the way back then. And back on Moya, a couple of times she quickly smiles at him, or holds his gaze just a little bit too long... I knew if I planted a couple of seeds like that, the writers would pick up on it, and they did. They ran with the baton!"

The writers increasingly put Sikozu and Scorpius together, which greatly pleased Hill. "I love watching Wayne work," she says. "It's great fun, He's like a dancer. He's very artistic. He can tilt his head and look at you in a particular way, and he doesn't need to say anything. It's all there in the look. He knows that mask so well now. He knows exactly what picture the audience is going to get if he turns his head slightly this way, or that way. He knows every crevice. And he *works* it. He's unashamed. He puts it right out there!"

Although Hill was delighted that Sikozu and Scorpius left Moya together, albeit involuntarily, her parting from the other characters didn't match her expectations. "I was disappointed she didn't get more of an opportunity to sever her ties with Aeryn in particular," Hill says. "They'd become quite close and depended on each other back in 'Bringing Home the Beacon'. Claudia and I never had any intention of having any bitchiness or cattiness there. We wanted two females together that could have a normal friendship like two male figures. But on that final day of filming, there just wasn't any time. Claudia and I tried to insert a few looks here and there, but we couldn't get one line thrown in to soften the departure a bit. I had a lot of problems with the last couple of episodes, actually. Sikozu was their ally all through the season and suddenly there's no farewell, no rationale for throwing her off, nothing. Because Scorpius was screwing her, it was goodbye!"

Hill was looking forward to finding out what happened between Sikozu and Scorpius on Braca's Command Carrier during the fifth season. "I would have been much more comfortable off Moya than on, I think, and I'm sure that they would have come back as the Prince and Princess of Darkness in the fifth season," she says. "I understood Scorpius. I knew where he was coming from. He made the most sense to me of everybody on that show. I would have loved to have come back and played with him. It's so upsetting and frustrating that there's no resolution. We're just left dangling. That final shot is so damn infuriating!" ■

" In my time as Dominar, some of my actions resulted in the deaths of the undeserving. Even when the cause is just, it's a hard thing to accept."

Jonathan Hardy considers that Rygel "is far more than just a puppet from a mould. It's a bit like any human being — they may have incredibly annoying aspects, but when it's called out of them, they are actually there for you. That's what I'm most proud of and delighted with. Rygel isn't a leading man type. He isn't a character performance. To paraphrase Shakespeare, he is unto himself truthful, and that is remarkable for a puppet... In fact, I don't think of him as a puppet at all!"

So how would Hardy describe him? "The two most intelligent people on that ship are Scorpius and Rygel," he states. "He is not a 'Buckwheat', or whatever names Crichton might come up. He is not a selfish little man, nor is he a great or a bad ruler. He is Rygel. Different sides of him are drawn forth by what he is reacting to: sometimes he has to be greedy and sometimes self-serving, sometimes heroic, sometimes politically very astute and game-playing. He is clever, cowardly and brave. He's obviously a considerably persuasive creature. The great thing about him is that he is never simply a particular 'type'."

The Dominar reminds Hardy of some of the great actors of recent times, such as Laurence Olivier and Anthony Hopkins. "With all great acting there seems to be something in reserve," he says. "There seems to be a mind and a soul out of which the replies are coming. The replies are particular to that situation, but something inside is watching... With Rygel, you're not getting the totality of the person, but you know it's there."

During the fourth year, the puppetry team changed the way they operated, and Fiona Gentile succeeded Tim Mieville as Rygel's on-set voice for the last third of the season, although she had been part of Team Rygel through the year. "Rygel had some rather soft moments at the beginning of the year," she notes. "There were some amazingly beautiful scenes with Elack's Pilot. Rygel rarely shows his softer side and his gruff kindness, but we've seen that in scenes with Noranti."

Gentile also found Rygel's reaction to the Charrids in 'Mental as Anything' very revealing. Once again, the Charrids brought out a tougher side to the Dominar. "That's the first time he's faced the enemy on his terms. He knows he's going to get hurt, and he usually runs away from that," she notes. "He had an amazing speech about exactly what the Charrids had done to him and his race. He's always felt responsible for the fact that his race was attacked and overtaken by the Charrids, and hundreds of thousands

were killed. As the Dominar, he was unable to protect them. He had one of those truthful moments with D'Argo when he berates himself for being such a failure — how could he let everyone be slaughtered? It was a huge, 'I've got to face this now or never face it' moment. That was a really important scene for him in the season. It's a shame it was cut from the broadcast version, though it's going to be on the DVD."

The practicalities of operating Rygel presented their usual difficulties, and on a number of occasions during the year, Mat McCoy was called upon to demonstrate his art of 'hide-ology'. "If it's a really wide shot, we can use the animatronic puppet without the data cables, or just use the dummy," McCoy explains, "but the dummy puppet, well, it looks like a dummy! The job for us throughout the season was trying to find ways to get me out of the camera's way, so we could avoid having to use the dummy puppet. It was always a problem for the actors working opposite Rygel as well. Animatronic puppets of Rygel's complexity have five or seven people operating them! Who should they talk to, and how do they interact? The obvious answer was that they acted with the puppet as if it was an actor, but it would be a shock to the system for them if they didn't realise what was involved from our side."

The puppeteers also faced a new situation with Rygel in 'Unrealized Reality', as their Hynerian developed Luxan tendencies. "When you design

a puppet, it's got certain parameters," Mat McCoy says. "Rygel moves in a certain way, partly because I move that way, but also because he's locked down in a throne sled. It was a challenge to try and get a different kind of energy out of him. We had to take this perfect diplomat, ready to sell out anyone for his own good, and turn him into a dwarfish Luxan warrior who's ready to kill them all!"

As an actor, Hardy enjoyed the sonorous nature of some of Rygel's lines. "You couldn't speak that dialogue, you had to open your throat and *utter* it," he smiles. "You're using the language as words of power." The challenge for him, as always, was making it appear as if he had been voicing Rygel on set. "The great thing I enjoyed about doing Rygel was listening to what the other actor had said, without the other actor being there in the booth with me, and accurately replying — but also making that reply fit what the puppeteers had done, sometimes quite independently of the guide vocal track that we had," he recalls. "Often the guide track would go one way, and we'd take a completely different reading. Sometimes the puppeteers were just reading the lines, but of course they were under considerable pressure to get everything done on the studio floor."

As far as Hardy was concerned, that was why he and sound engineer Angus Robertson spent their time working on the episodes. "There was a philosophy to what we were doing," he explains. "Acting is reacting, and the performance never lies with the individual. It lies between the two actors. Controlling that 'interspace' between two people is at the heart of any art form. We were trying to create an interspace between me and the other actor, even if they were not there, and we only had their image to work with. Rygel's image was committed, but his voice wasn't, so we could create that interspace.

"Rygel was a genuine person," Hardy adds, "more genuine than a lot of the flesh and blood characters." The actor has very happy memories of his four years providing the voice for the Hynerian, and to the very last day working with Angus Robertson, he kept one tenet in mind. "When David Kemper and I spoke about him, it was in terms of him being that which he reacted to. He's a great piece of characterisation. You know, I always come back to Hamlet when I describe him. Hamlet himself remains a mystery, and so to an extent does Rygel!" ∎

"We cannot serve so many masters at once. We ask you to choose one spokesperson."

here were so many characters to service on *Farscape* this year, Pilot did occasionally get overlooked," says Lani Tupu, who provided the voice of Moya's Pilot throughout the series. "You almost go back to season one, where nothing much happens. In many ways, he's just reacting."

Puppeteer Fiona Gentile, who was part of Team Pilot as well as Team Rygel, felt that "he was a lot more sombre this year. I talked to producer Ricky Manning about him, because I was interested in what was happening to Pilot. I wouldn't say that he exactly grew up, but he was definitely a lot less naïve in this season, and a lot less willing to take on everybody else's crazy plans and stupid ideas."

Although Gentile feels that Pilot was a "bit more assertive", Tupu thinks that could have gone a lot further. He was surprised by Pilot's decision to ask the crew to choose a captain from amongst themselves at the end of 'Promises'. "I would have wanted him to have been much more pro-active," he says. "I could see opportunities in there for the writers to push it a little in certain places, because Pilot would have heard everything on board, and at least made some kind of comment about it. They were space babies from his point of view. But that never happened."

It is gradually revealed that between seasons, Pilot and Moya were interrogated by the Einstein figure that John Crichton later encounters inside the wormhole in 'Unrealized Reality'. This leaves both Pilot and Moya fearful of wormholes, and Crichton has to encourage them to help him with his research. By the end of the year, Crichton desperately needs their help in order to carry out his plan to save Earth, and, after some encouragement from Rygel, Pilot eventually agrees.

"What he did was amazing," Fiona Gentile says. "He was willing to be transplanted into the transport pod, knowing how much pain that would cause. He was willing to risk his life for his friends and be parted from Moya. It showed a much more mature outlook. I've always felt there was a real depth to Pilot, but in making that decision at the end, he was taking responsibility for Crichton, even though Crichton had always been the one to lead him into these crazy schemes and get him into trouble! I thought that made a lovely ending with him making this gesture."

Tupu agrees. "I don't think the writers knew when they were creating 'Bad Timing' that the show would actually finish, but giving him the line 'Thank you' to say in that episode was one of the most pleasurable

lines I've had to deliver on behalf of Pilot. That wrapped the whole *Farscape* story up for me, from his point of view. Throughout that episode, I had a collection of lines that just felt so good when I said them. It really wrapped up the character's journey: who he was, in terms of being the navigator, going through all those experiences like having his arm chopped off, not to mention bollocking everyone on the ship! For him to say 'thank you' at the end was like a completion."

'Bad Timing' also presented Tupu with a vocal challenge. "I had to make Pilot's screams different from Crais's screams," he says, recalling the times in which he had been put in torment in his on-screen role. "If you go back and listen really carefully to Pilot's screams earlier in the series, like in 'DNA Mad Scientist' when his arm's chopped off, the vocal range is completely different, which makes the screams totally different. That was really tricky, because in that last episode, I had to scream for about a minute and a half, which is quite a long time! We had to do that about five or six times, and it was really difficult getting back into it. But Angus Robertson is a fantastic ADR technician, and he kept me on track. Over the four years, he gave me so much direction and help."

Tupu had to cope with different people handling Pilot's mouth and voice on set, after Sean Masterson's departure midway through the season,

and Peter Jagger's arrival as puppetry co-ordinator. "Sean had a deliberate pace, which was just the way he spoke, I guess," Tupu explains. "But it also meant he slowed down quite a lot and I could actually synchronise my dialogue to his movement. When Mario Halouvas took over that aspect of Pilot, he spoke very fast, and was very different from the way that I would say Pilot's lines. I sometimes had to turn down the guide track and try to sync it up visually on screen. Even with Sean, the challenge had been to forget the rhythms he used, and put my own — or Pilot's — rhythms in there. It was a bit difficult when it was chopping and changing. Maybe it would have been easier if someone had just said them in a neutral way."

Above: Elack's elderly Pilot.

The writers placed a number of scenes in Pilot's Den during the year. "Mario always said that there was a time when nobody dared step inside Pilot's Inner Sanctum," Fiona Gentile recalls, "and then the directors cottoned on to the fact that it worked incredibly well to have the other characters up close to him, because of the size difference. There were times when we had Rygel and Pilot together. Rygel needs seven puppeteers, and Pilot has five — and we were all in Pilot's tiny little space. At one point, one of the male puppeteers said to me that if I moved my head a fraction, we'd have to get married! My head was not where it was meant to be! It felt like we were doing a full-on game of Twister underneath there sometimes."

Pilot wouldn't necessarily react the same way twice, so the puppeteers never felt that they were providing 'stock' reactions. "In 'Natural Election'," Mat McCoy recalls, "Pilot was unconscious, but there are gradients of unconsciousness. We had to work out how to maintain that. We tried to work out how this invasion of his body would affect Pilot. We could never just whip out 'expression E17'!"

Although Tupu feels there is an element of closure for Pilot in 'Bad Timing', he still wishes there had been a fifth season, with opportunities to explore other avenues. "But in a strange way, the ending, which leaves everything hanging in the air, is perfect *Farscape*," he adds.

Fiona Gentile speaks for the entire puppetry team, if not the entire cast when she says, "I have a wealth of amazing and fun memories. What a joy to be able to play with such imaginative characters! I'm exceedingly grateful to have had that job." ∎

David Kemper

" This is a show where you can do anything. We realised that our actors are unafraid, and whenever we get that, we start tossing great stuff at them."

Commandant Mele-On **Grayza** first appears in season three's 'Into The Lion's Den', taking Scorpius to task for his obsession with John Crichton and wormholes. In the course of her brief meeting with Crichton, she begins to understand why Scorpius is so fascinated by this human, and as the fourth season progresses, she too comes to recognise Crichton as a formidable opponent.

Grayza was born on a Command Carrier and has achieved the pinnacle of Peacekeeper advancement, beginning as a Strategic Tactician and rising rapidly through the ranks, until Captain, Vice Admiral and even Admiral rank could not hold her. She is now a Flag Officer of the highest station within the military establishment. Relentlessly dogged, cool and determined, she has never met her match in anyone. Her self-confidence projects itself like a bow wake washing over all who come in contact with her. When alpha individuals enter a room other alphas often rise to the challenge; with Grayza, however, her force is such that most rivals submit without conflict, realising success would elude them. She is endowed with a physical and psychological understanding of people in situations. Well-educated, cultured and ruthless, she still sees herself as being on the way up. She is quite comfortable with the notion that she could be the top of the Sebacean Empire.

Grayza

" Perhaps Scorpius's enemy will be my friend."

Rebecca Riggs has thoroughly enjoyed playing the part, which was described in her character brief as 'without doubt, the most dangerous person we've ever met.' "She is very different to Scorpius, who is incredibly determined and ruthless as well," Riggs explains. "But Scorpius is a monster who looks like a monster, whereas she is a monster who can seem like a diplomat — but she is a monster nevertheless! She's never found anybody that was worth connecting to. Her path forward in life has been extremely easy, which makes her much more likely to despise the people around her."

Grayza is willing to use any weapon at her disposal, including what the *Farscape* crew referred to as her "titty swipe". "She has a gland which secretes something which can basically turn men to putty," Riggs smiles. "It comes onto her body, and one whiff of that, they're gone!" When she uses it on Crichton in 'What Was Lost', the human believes he has been

raped. "I don't think she thinks it's rape," Riggs counters. "I don't think she would truly understand that crime. Sex is a different act in her culture. She was getting information from him in a way that has worked many times before, and is actually painless."

Riggs loved working with David Franklin, relishing the 'double act' of Grayza and Braca. "It was fantastic from the first day," she says. "We had a very good time, especially when the scripts were turning up seconds before we went on! We had enough faith and joy in each other to go wherever was necessary. You know, as far as I'm concerned, *Farscape* was really *The Grayza and Braca Show*!"

One of the reasons Rebecca Riggs wanted to work on *Farscape* was to interact with the character of **Braca**, who she foresaw would go from a position of subservience to ruling the universe. David Franklin enjoyed Braca's continued rise during the fourth season, which culminated in Scorpius handing Grayza's Command Carrier over to him at the end of the year. "What's been interesting for me is developing Braca from Mr Brownnose," Franklin explains. "He has an arc. He's matured a lot, and he's capable of making his own decisions. Where do his loyalties lie? He's capable of being a captain now, whereas two years ago, there was no way

you could say that. I'm glad he's not the same Sebacean he was when he started out. As an actor, I would have been very bored!"

Franklin knew from the start of the year that Braca was Scorpius's spy on board Grayza's ship. "That was the old double-triple-quadruple whammy cross!" he jokes. "I had to look after Scorpy. It was like Braca was screwing Grayza all the time. She's like a black widow spider — and that analogy isn't hard to miss with her in that chair. It was quite satisfying for him to be outwitting her, except for the bumps and grazes along the way. But I loved working with Rebecca!"

One of those bumps and grazes involved being possessed by the Skreeth in 'Terra Firma'. "I'm sure Braca was thinking, 'Hang on, this wasn't in the deal!' Things were always in danger of getting away from him," Franklin says. "On the one hand, he had the feeling of control, but it was only an illusion. Where was his back-up? Where was his support? He was definitely on his own out there."

Franklin claims he didn't know how he was going to play the Skreeth until the camera started rolling. "On *Farscape*, you've just got to commit to whatever choice you make," he points out. "I couldn't recall ever having been possessed by a Skreeth before. I scanned my memories and couldn't find it — perhaps it was so traumatic that I blocked it out! Seriously though, I just went to town. I joked about it before and after, but when you're actually doing it, you really *are* being taken over by a Skreeth!"

Franklin was looking forward to the fifth year, to see where the Scorpius/Sikozu/Braca triangle would go: "At the end of the fourth year, he had that moment where he's watching them. There was the

Scorpius to Braca

" I'm not given to exaggeration, but the future of Peacekeeper survival depends on you."

voyeuristic attraction of watching a private moment, and he must also have been wondering: is this relationship of theirs going to be threatening to me? Where do I stand in this? It would have been nice to have had season five, but that's life in the big city..."

The crew of Moya bids farewell to **Jool** (or to give her full name, Joolushko Tunai Fenta Hovalis) at the end of the two-parter early in the

fourth year, 'What Was Lost', although there were plans to bring the character back during the fifth season. Tammy MacIntosh, who had moved over to work on the Australian medical drama *All Saints*, found the parting bittersweet.

"You start acting because you get to be a kid, and you get to play and have fun," she points out. "Everyone who starts acting says it's not really a job, then as you get older you realise that it is, and you start to be sensible about it. And then you come across *Farscape*, and the whole thing gets turned on its head. You get sent back to when you were fifteen and it's so much fun — *and* you're being paid!"

After the problems she experienced during the third season, MacIntosh found the make-up process much easier for her reappearances in these episodes, and in the alternate worlds of 'John Quixote' and 'Unrealized Reality'. "I thought she was much more striking in the final episodes," she says. "We changed the look of her eyes, and what was on her lids. We finally decided to stay with the red wig. It became an aesthetic thing, especially with the introduction of Sikozu, who was very similar in colour to Jool's original look. It felt like my skin had finally got the gig, and we had worked out everything for my face. For those episodes, everything felt really calm, really good. I had no problems."

MacIntosh believes that calmness was reflected in the character. "It felt like she had come into herself after her experiences on Moya," she explains. "The aesthetic look came about as she finally arrived at a place where she had an opportunity to go home. At the same time, she realised how much she had learned, and how much she had grown to love the people on Moya. After all her initial experiences of frustration, not wanting to be there and absolutely hating the place, it was nice to be in a situation where she finally appreciated the efforts, the integrity, the courage and the camaraderie of everyone on Moya. It took her a very long time to just stop, and take a look at herself. It was only when she was rescued from something and told to shut up that she realised. It's very evident that everyone had come to recognise each other, love each other and wish each other the absolute best for what was coming in the future."

Jool

"I always wait. You know, see both sides. Be reasonable. But now, I have nothing to lose."

Although Crichton and Chiana encounter what David Kemper describes as a "raving psychotic" version of **Stark** within the game in 'John Quixote', the crew doesn't meet the real former Banik slave until the end of their battle on Katratzi in 'We're So Screwed'. Emperor Staleek creates a Bioloid replica of Stark to torture Scorpius in 'Hot to Katratzi', who then battles Noranti and Rygel as they seek to save the real Stark in 'La Bomba'.

Paul Goddard took this potentially bewildering array of Starks in his stride. Indeed, he was upset that he only had one opportunity to play the nasty side of the Bioloid. "I would have liked to bring that change about when I stopped torturing Scorpy and was talking to Ahkna, but Ahkna didn't know he was a Bioloid, so I had to continue to be the Bioloid pretending to be the real Stark," he explains. "There was no other opportunity to switch! The only time you saw the 'real' Bioloid was when he was about to be killed!"

A number of scenes featuring the genuine Stark didn't reach the final cut of the last episode. They would have revealed some hints about what had happened to him since the end of 'The Choice', and also what was in store for him in the fifth season. "I think he'd been through a bit of hell, and been here, there and everywhere," Goddard speculates. "In 'John Quixote', we learn that in order to get some money, he sold part of his memories to the game-maker. At some point he lost Zhaan's voice, and then he was just aimless. As long as he could hear Zhaan's voice, he had some point, but when it ceased to exist for him, maybe that's when he got caught by the Scarrans. I think they did some very bad things to him, and pushed him to the edge again. He was so happy to be back on Moya, and to be useful. Well, he thought so, although I don't think he was particularly useful, actually!"

Noranti to Stark
"Troubled Stykera, float on memories, and perhaps time will heal your wounds."

Stark's pleasure reflected the actor's joy at returning to *Farscape*. "It was so good to be back playing with everybody," Goddard recalls. "I felt like it was all beginning again. David Kemper and I talked about the damage that had been wrought on Stark this time, and how he would change the way he expressed it. He never laughed very much before that, so now he had fits of hysterical laughter. We thought of different ways in which he would be derailing and disruptive, rather than just making huge mistakes. We had great plans, but it was not to be!" ■

THE EFFECTS

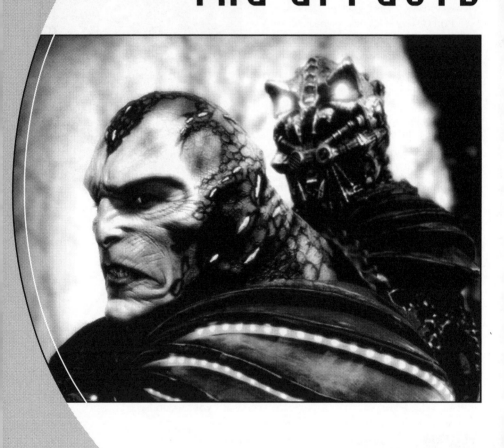

" Tonight, we will pierce the veil of secrecy, showing you these aliens as no one has witnessed them before."

– R. Wilson Monroe

Raelee Hill

" These days who says, 'When I'm a grown up, I want to be a puppeteer.' Who does that? Only crazy people. The Creature Shop
crew are gorgeous, but they are the maddest bunch!"

W e hit the ground running this year," says Dave Elsey. For the Creature
Shop creative supervisor and his crew, there wasn't much time
between the start of pre-production and the beginning of filming on
season four. Retaining most of the personnel who had worked on the
third season, Elsey added a few key people, assigning dedicated teams to the various characters.

"We wanted each character to be looked after by a solid crew of people,"
Elsey's colleague Colin Ware explains. "The same people would do all the
seaming of the appliances for 'their' character, do the pre-painting, and fit them
to the mechanisms where necessary. They'd apply them each morning, and
then stay with the characters on set. It gave us some quality control all the way
through. It sounds relatively easy, but we had to break down all the schedules
and work out how many times each character had to be on set. Then we could
make sure we had enough skins ready."

Elsey brought in specialists in hair and make-up, who ensured that both
D'Argo's and Noranti's hair looked more natural. "D'Argo's hair never really
looked real," Elsey notes, "which always irritated us. It's meant to be straight,
but before season four it had been pretty lifeless."

Now that Noranti was a regular character on *Farscape*, Elsey appointed
Katherine Brown as her make-up artist. "She was a revelation — a fantastic
make-up artist who was also interested in prosthetics, and had done a little bit
of that under her own steam," Elsey recalls. "She was comfortable with the air-
brush and the handbrush, and then we handed her the remote control handset
to work Noranti's third eye on set, and she did that as well!"

Rygel remained much the same as previously, although Elsey and his
team worked on improving the Dominar's smile. "The servos can move the
smile and the face around into quite absurd positions!" Elsey grins.

Pilot underwent a number of changes. The original Pilot body had been
created in London by Jamie Courtier, before *Farscape* began shooting in 1998.
It was now coming to the end of its useful life, and the Creature Shop took
advantage of the absence of Moya to work on the new skin. For the first three
episodes, they had to create an alternate, elderly Pilot to run Elack, so they used
the rotting foam from the original Pilot while working on its replacement.
Pilot's physical absence in 'Lava's a Many Splendored Thing' allowed them to
complete the work.

The largest changes were to Scorpius, because of the problems caused by

the sudden dramatic weight loss that Wayne Pygram was suffering. "He was becoming thinner and thinner, and suddenly nothing was fitting," Elsey recalls. "His make-up was starting to look incredibly good, though!"

"The fit of the helmet is really quite critical to keep all the bits round his mouth in place," Colin Ware adds. "They are not glued on: there's just a zip up the back which holds everything in place. We had to do a whole new reworking of the helmet. It was an absolute pain to get right."

The Creature Shop created another version of Scorpius for 'Promises', in which Claudia Black had to appear in the hybrid's costume. "The suit was specially made for her," Elsey notes, "as were the helmet and make-up. We'd been rather too successful hiding Ben inside the make-up when he played Crichton/Scorpius, so we did a 'prettier' version, so you could see Claudia through it. She didn't find the helmet very comfortable, so we had to reinvent it, and changed over from solid plastic earpieces to little foam latex ones that were formed around her head and ears."

When Wayne Pygram adjusted his diet, and began to put weight back on, the Creature Shop crew made further adjustments to his costume, giving him the foam latex earpieces as well. These could still have the LED lights imbedded in them, but were far more comfortable for the actor to wear. "Wayne was very grateful for the extra room in the helmet," Elsey recalls. "He has a constant ringing in his ears due to the fact he plays the drums a lot in his spare time, and it wasn't getting any better listening to his own voice going around his head."

Although the producers ultimately decided to define Sikozu's appearance with make-up only, Elsey was involved in discussions about her look, particularly as the producers already knew that she would be revealed to be a robot later in the season. "We talked a lot about the robots in the Steven Spielberg film *A.I.*," Elsey says. "I said that we ought to make her perfect." The various solutions that were discussed would be helpful later in the year, when Aeryn Sun turns out to be a Bioloid replacement in 'Bringing Home the Beacon'.

Elsey recalls there was one other major development in the Creature Shop's work for the fourth year: "We started to create more background aliens for scenes. We decided that we needed to find a way of populating the universe with more aliens that could do a little bit. We found a great way of making lots of background masks. We only needed to do one initial sculpture, but then each mask would end up looking slightly different. We could have one main member of the species, and then some background grunts to carry the suitcases, as it were!"

The Creature Shop was not able to call on the talents of Thomas Holesgrove to play the aliens in the fourth year, as he had moved away from Australia. Some other *Farscape* veterans stepped in however, including John Adam, who had played the Tavlek Bekhesh in the first two seasons. He returned to play Raa'Keel, the Tarkan smuggler in 'Lava's A Many Splendored Thing'. "It's always good to go with someone who can deal with this kind of thing, rather than launch in with somebody new who's never worn it before," Elsey comments. "It's not as easy as pulling on a hat. With the head design we were using, I knew we were going to lose the actor's eyes for this role, and it was going to be difficult for him. John had been nearly blind as Bekhesh, and we seized the opportunity to make him blind again!"

Elsey enjoyed creating the alien suit, which was partially inspired by the costumes designed for the Judge Dredd strip in the British comic *2000 AD*. "The helmet was intrinsic to the head," he explains. "I like costumes where you don't see the eyes. I think it's great on a villain. The helmet went on magnetically and it was vacuformed. It was like a pair of mirror sunglasses: we had it vacuum metallised, so John could just about see out, but we couldn't see in. That was fairly successful, although we ended up making some adjustments to it due to the weirdness of the set. There was not a straight edge on the whole of that lava planet! John was walking down little narrow alleyways, which were only about a foot wide with lava on both sides, so it became necessary to give him better vision."

Not for the first time, the imaginations of the writers were piqued by the creature design. "The make-up for Raa'Keel's face worked well, but it was tricky to do," Elsey recalls. "We put big teeth in John Adam's mouth, and pushed his lips out as far as we possibly could. The lip piece went over the top of his nose, so you couldn't see where his nose was meant to be. David Kemper and Andrew Prowse were fascinated by this, but they really wanted to see the creature's eyes. I had to tell them that there was nothing under the helmet — I hadn't made anything!"

Nevertheless, the producers were determined to see the Tarkan without his headgear. "I knew it wouldn't work as a make-up, so we made big eyes that went on the side of the head and made him look much more alien," Elsey says. "It made much more sense out of his profile. When Raa'Keel took his helmet

Page 133: Team Scorpius: (clockwise from top): Wayne Pygram, Colin Ware, Kerrin Jackson and Dave Elsey.

Opposite page: The Aeryn/Scorpius hybrid.

Above: Raa'Keel hides his eyes from view.

off to reveal his eyes, all you in fact revealed were two inner helmets on John Adam's head!"

The idea of removing a creature's helmet to see what was underneath stayed with the writers, and they made it a key plot point four episodes later, in 'I Shrink Therefore I Am'. When the bounty hunter leader Axikor removes his helmet, we are treated to our first glimpse of a Brain Scarran, the new type of the breed created for the series' fourth year.

"I coined the term Brain Scarran," Dave Elsey explains. "When it comes to the Scarrans, I've always seen 'the bigger picture', and thought there should be different versions of them: some that are more human, and others more animalistic; a whole evolutionary scale. I talked about that with David Kemper, and he started to make it part of the story."

This different kind of Scarran could be created with make-up appliances, rather than full animatronics. "At the beginning of the season I did a maquette of a Brain Scarran showing what we could potentially do," Elsey says. "Everyone loved it, and I thought it was still Scarran-y enough, and hopefully was the right blend of things. We'd already seen the more humanoid and less scaly version with a smaller head and more human proportions during the third season, so we were already heading in that direction."

Initially the bounty hunters in 'I Shrink Therefore I Am' were conceptualised as huge creatures, big enough to imprison a full-size member of the crew inside them. "They were going to be giant walking refrigerators," Elsey recalls, "large, lightweight constructions that looked as if they were made of rusted metal. Luckily, somebody saw the light just before we started building them, and suggested miniaturising everyone instead!"

But Elsey still had to create a race of robots. "Robots are one of the most difficult things to do on science fiction television, which explains why they've been done so unsuccessfully before," he points out. "On a film, you can spend months perfecting suits and polishing each piece. We only had two weeks, so instead, we decided to do rusty, dirty, grubby soldiers, and make them more biomechanical."

Elsey took inspiration from the British sci-fi institution *Doctor Who* to help identify which bounty hunter was talking, since the suits themselves had no mouthpieces. "We used the idea of the lights flashing on the creature's head,

Opposite page: The bounty hunter Axikor.

Above: Another of the Creature Shop's triumphs — the marine dwelling Oo-Nii from 'What Was Lost'.

like the Daleks," he says. "They were operated automatically by the actors' voices, which was difficult to do because we didn't want the microphone to pick up their breathing, and have the lights flashing away the whole time!"

The Creature Shop crew sculpted the sections of the bounty hunters' bodies, and then tailored them to fit each of the actors who would be wearing them. "The suits were quite a major deal in terms of what was going on in them," Elsey notes. "There were all the electronics and the lights. We had lights under the ribcages and under the arms as well as in the head."

The hunters were also armed. "That was a last minute addition," Elsey recalls. "We had made a mechanical gauntlet with an injector device that came out, and we added a knife. We ran into problems with the safety officer, who didn't want it to be pointed. Eventually we came to a compromise and made a real knife for close-ups, and then a soft one from rubber. You couldn't tell the difference actually — and for the record, there were no accidents with either!"

Elsey also had to create the bounty hunters' innards. "David Kemper wanted the inside of their bodies to resemble pumpkin flesh," the designer recalls. "We got through so much tinted KY jelly on *Farscape!*"

For the first time in *Farscape*'s history, these were suits that also included their own self-contained air conditioning, which made life immeasurably easier for the actors working in the baking Sydney heat. "Flick a button, and they could cool themselves down," Elsey explains. "Before then, we had to run over in between takes and turn on the fans, but now they were like astronauts — they could wear the costumes all the time, and walk around in complete comfort. In fact, we were often asked to turn them down because people were getting too cold!"

Axikor was played by Duncan Young, who would return to play the Scarran Emperor Staleek in the closing episodes of the season. "Duncan was instantly bigger and better than anyone else in the bounty hunter suits," Dave Elsey says. "You immediately knew it was him, even though they were all very similar. He loved being in the make-up and he could act in it. He could bring a completely lifeless suit alive."

The Scarrans dominated the last third of the season, as Crichton and the Moya crew travel to Katratzi in search of Aeryn. 'Bringing Home the Beacon' introduced another new type of Scarran — the predatory female, Ahkna, played by Ben Browder's wife, Francesca Buller. Buller had made an appearance in each previous season wearing different prosthetics and make-ups, from the calcium-seeking M'Lee in the first year's 'Bone to be Wild', via the impish Jakench Ro-Na in the 'Look at the Princess' trilogy, to the unscrupulous Raxil in 'Scratch 'n' Sniff' in year three.

"The producers came to me and asked who they should cast as the Scarran female," Dave Elsey remembers. "I said that we needed a tall, statuesque person, and they then told me they were thinking about bringing in

Above: Minister Ahkna and Captain Jenek.

Fran. I thought that was a great idea, but Fran isn't tall — she's actually very small. When they asked how that would affect it, I pointed out that, basically, she would be shorter than the others!"

As ever on *Farscape*, the Creature Shop crew met the challenge head on. "We figured that if Fran was going to be the smallest Scarran, she needed to have the biggest hat! [Fabrication supervisor] Lou Elsey designed an outrageously brilliant costume for her. Fran had played a lot of androgynous roles on the show, but she had never got to play sexy. She wanted to know if we could make this character sexy, and we pointed out that as far as we are concerned, *all* the Scarrans are sexy. In fact, they're the sexiest things we've ever done on the show!"

After a shopping expedition with the fabrication supervisor, Buller's fears were laid to rest when she found the costume for Ahkna. "We worked closely with her, getting the body language right," Dave Elsey adds. "It's amazing how much better she was at dealing with the 'high heels' than any of the blokes — but the men in the Scarran suits took it as a challenge to be able to walk in heels as well as her!"

The Creature Shop spent a long time working on the different Scarran costumes for the assorted members of the race. "Jason Clarke played Jenek, who was the first of the other Scarrans we see in their full regalia," Elsey recalls. "We put a lot of effort into the detail on the Scarran costumes. The Creature Shop is a great department to do costumes in, because we have access to many more materials than the usual costume department would have. We can even create our own fabrics. We can also go further with the armour than most costume departments on a television show would ever be able to."

To create all the Scarrans that were needed for the final episodes, the Creature Shop was running at a manic pace. "We were getting conflicting information on the numbers that were required," Colin Ware recalls. "On one day we'd be told there'd only be one coming up, then we'd be told there were going to be ten, or six, or five. But once you've started building six, you're building six. We had suits coming out every five minutes! We had to create all the bits and pieces — the moulds, the armour, the make-ups. We were going flat out."

Once filming began, things were even more hectic. "We had five or six make-ups to do one after the other," Ware adds. "Scorpius would normally take us forty-five minutes to an hour to create. On some days that was pulled back to half an hour, just because there was no other way to do it and still get everyone ready on set. We had people standing up from the chair and there would be someone else sitting down before the first person had been finished off."

"We had make-up Scarrans, animatronic Scarrans and background Scarrans, with the idea being that they would be at different levels of complexity," Elsey continues. "But that turned out to be an absolute fallacy — they were all as difficult as each other to build, and all as complicated. We had to do body movement tests with the actors as well. We had to train up the actors to move fluidly in heels. We got our mechanical guy, Sonny Tilders, to work on the lip and facial mechanisms of the animalistic Scarrans, and he really got the necks moving around very fluidly."

The Creature Shop crew had one more challenge coming up. "We knew we were going to meet the Emperor, and that the Emperor was going to be played by Duncan Young, and that he was going to be great," Elsey states. Before Elsey saw the scripts for the final episodes, he and Wayne Pygram had been discussing where the series seemed to be heading, and both thought it was probable that there would be a confrontation between Scorpius and the Scarran Emperor. "We figured the Emperor had to be the biggest Scarran you've ever seen," Elsey explains. "We'd build it as a big mechanical puppet — we wouldn't be able to do it any other way. We really tried hard to do that, but the producers didn't let us — luckily, as it turned out, because we had so much other stuff to do! But we did end up meeting the ultimate Scarran."

Lou Elsey worked solidly for forty-eight hours before Duncan Young stepped onto set, to ensure the costume was exactly right. "We wanted it to be

Opposite page: The ultimate Scarran — Emperor Staleek.

different," Dave Elsey explains. "Everything about him was going to be red. All the Scarrans we'd seen so far wore various shades of black, silver and gold — very muted colours. When we meet the Emperor, he's clearly got the textile mills going full pelt making his gear, and he's got the best of everything! We even built a sword for him, but he didn't end up using that."

The costume was completed literally ten minutes before Young was required in front of the cameras. There was no time for any changes, even if any had been needed. "We were thrilled," Elsey recalls. "The whole shop was tired, but everyone was buzzing with excitement. We aimed way too high with the Scarrans really, but we pulled it off. I think they're beautiful, and I don't think there's ever been anything like them before in a science fiction show, in terms of their detail and core quality. We're very proud that we were lucky enough to get to do the costumes on the Scarrans, too. We worked hard to make those creatures look good. They were worthy bad guys."

The final creation of the Creature Shop came right at the very end of 'Bad Timing', with the Qujagan pilot of the ship that neutralises Crichton and Aeryn for inspection. The crew were asked not to do anything too outlandish, as it was planned that the race would reappear at the start of the fifth season. "They had to be something we could do as make-ups," Colin Ware recalls.

"We knew this was going to be the last alien we saw on the show this season," Dave Elsey continues. "But I didn't want it to be a make-up — I wanted it to be more interesting. I came up with the idea of these people who I dubbed the Jigsaw Men. They were made of little squares, and could take themselves apart, and put themselves back together in whatever form they needed to do whatever they were doing. They could look humanoid most of the time."

The advantage of this approach, Elsey reckoned, was that you didn't need to actually see every member of the race change — but each time you saw one, you knew he might be able to if necessary. "I discussed it with Colin and Sonny Tilders, and between us we came up with the idea that he'd be driving his spaceship, and his boss would say, 'Have you got them in your sights?' He'd look out of the window, and say, 'Hang on a minute.' Then his head would open up, and a whole new set of eyes would come out. Then he'd say, 'Yes, I've got them in my sights!'"

Elsey realised the pilot didn't actually need to be done as a make-up at all — the part could be played by a puppet. "You were only ever going to see him from the waist up, so it was perfect," he recalls. "Sonny was brilliant, and devised a mechanism which had perfect lip synchronisation on the lower half, and the eyes and brows worked on the upper half, and then the thing split open and a whole new set of eyes appeared. It could all be synchronised on the computer, and done in one shot. Terry Ryan created the costume (which I thought looked like that 1980s pop band, Sigue Sigue Sputnik), and it all came together rather quickly."

Sadly, the Qujagan was the last creation for *Farscape* from Elsey and his team. "I'm so happy that it is a memorable alien, and we ended with a scream, not a whimper," Elsey notes. "I'm so happy that it came from within the Creature Shop and it was our idea." "I don't think we would necessarily have done anything different if we had known the end was coming," Colin Ware adds.

If the series had continued with a fifth season, the Creature Shop crew were planning to renovate all of the main characters' make-ups, as well as introduce new computer controls to replace the systems that had been used since 1998. For the first year ever, Elsey also intended to retain all of the Creature Shop crew for a second consecutive season.

Looking back over the four years he was involved with the series, Elsey is full of praise for his co-workers, and the actors who went into make-up, or donned suits. "When it worked, it was *fantastic*," he says. "The things we put people through on *Farscape*! It was incredible. We were trying every idea we could possibly think of, doing stuff that most people would be happy to work on once in their careers — but we were doing it every single week! Above all though, we worked with such a great bunch of people, and that's what made it so special." ∎

Above: The Qujagan pilot in both his guises.

PRODUCTION DESIGN

"We were constantly building new sets during the fourth year. The art department was under extreme pressure. Tim Ferrier did the best job of the whole time he was on the show."

"Farscape gives me an opportunity just to go *mad*," designer Tim Ferrier explains. "Coming from reasonably straightforward television and features, to be given an opportunity where you can really do anything is just wonderful."

Tim Ferrier replaced Ricky Eyres as *Farscape*'s production designer early in the second season, starting his tenure with the outlandish sets for 'Picture If You Will'. As the show progressed, he was called upon to deliver increasingly complicated and strange environments, but they still had to be designs that the construction department could bring into reality at literally a week's notice.

Coming into the fourth season, Ferrier learned there were likely to be more episodes set on previously unseen alien planets, as Moya travelled out of the Uncharted Territories into Tormented Space. "That was a challenge, because it meant we'd have to create a new world every two weeks," he says. "As it turns out, things didn't eventuate quite as specifically as that."

Ferrier usually becomes involved with the scripts and storylines at a fairly early stage. "That's one of the great things about the show," he says. "We are told about the backstory of the planets we are visiting — not necessarily what is happening in the episode, but what has happened in the past. Everyone can throw in their ideas — Dave Elsey, costume designer Terry Ryan and I all have input into the history of the planet. Of course, sometimes logic prevails as well: if we can only do things a certain way, we'll twist the story a bit to fit that practicality."

If possible, Ferrier reuses existing sets. This doesn't simply apply to sets like the Moya corridors, which were redressed to become Elack in the first three episodes, and the marketplace in 'Bringing Home The Beacon'. For 'What Was Lost', Ferrier designed a domed set. "That turned up again in 'John Quixote', 'A Prefect Murder' and 'Kansas'," the designer recalls. "It actually got used more in 'John Quixote' than in the episode it was designed for: it was Claudia and Lani's bedroom, and also the room where Crichton and Chiana meet Stark."

What works well on paper, and is agreed at design stage by everyone involved from producer Andrew Prowse downwards, doesn't always translate into exactly the right idea when it's realised. 'John Quixote' demonstrated the need for flexibility. "We'd painted the room as a big dungeon,"

Ferrier says. "Andrew Prowse, director Tony Tilse and I were looking at it, just as it was nearly all finished, and I knew it wasn't working. Sometimes we have to go ahead and use something, even if it feels wrong, because we've simply run out of time. But on this occasion we still had a few days to go. I said, 'Wouldn't it be great if it was like a huge Magritte cloud painting?' I had to ask the painters to stop, and do it all as clouds. Their faces dropped, but they did it!"

Above: The production drawing for the marketplace seen in 'Bringing Home the Beacon'.

Sometimes a set is designed for only one episode, but will capture the writers' imaginations. "For 'Natural Election', we built what we all referred to as the scrubbing room, with those giant fans," Ferrier remembers. "It was easy to shoot in, and was good visually. If we had trouble working out where to put people, we'd set the scene there. It was a practical, utilitarian set, and easier to use than some others... so we never pulled it down. Whenever we'd be on the verge of striking it, the writers would set another scene there!"

One of Ferrier's favourite episodes in the fourth season was 'Mental as Anything', since it gave him the challenge of creating the arena, as well as giving a taste of Luxan architecture for the flashback sequences. "I loved the way that they cloaked a city in a tent of lights in the *Final Fantasy* movie," he explains. "That was the concept for the arena. There were technical queries about whether the lights would be bright enough, but our director of photography Russell Bacon just said, 'Let's try it!'"

When he was designing the Luxan home, Ferrier was conscious that he was creating the backstory for one of the central characters of the show. "There had never been any reference to the architecture or the style for D'Argo's planet," Ferrier notes. "Initially we thought it should have a Nordic feel to it, and we wanted to get away from the greys and blacks that we were using in the rest of the episode. It started off as a small set for two brief scenes, but it ended up being in eight or so huge scenes, so we had to enlarge it really quickly. The producers suggested we might do a whole episode on D'Argo's world in the fifth season."

Ferrier always enjoys creating an alien environment, and multiple episodes set in the same part of space give him a chance to expand his horizons. "David Kemper told me very early on in the year that towards the end of the season, we would be going to a Scarran base to rescue Scorpy, so I should plot towards creating that," Ferrier says. During the third season, Ferrier had designed sets that could be quickly redressed and reused to create the Command Carrier in the final episodes, and he

applied the same principle here, so that he wasn't designing Katratzi from scratch. "We started off with the transit station in 'Fetal Attraction', which was an airport lounge basically," he explains. "It had to have a lounge area, a medical room, a control room and a giant surgery. They were all redressed for the other episodes.

"We really reinforced what we had touched upon previously with Scarran architecture," he continues. "I wanted to use a lizard skin motif throughout, and orange and hot ochre colours to reflect the fact that Scarrans have a heat beam. Some of the ideas stemmed from what Dave Elsey and Terry Ryan had already done, and what we'd created for the Scarrans' props before now. We designed the conference room, the board table and chairs with all the jagged edges.

"They were a great set of episodes to finish with," Ferrier concludes. "I really got to design a whole world. Ongoing stuff is always the most satisfying — you know the sets are going to be there for a while, and they're going to be used a lot." ■

Opposite page: The Princess's bedchamber from 'John Quixote'.

Above: Design concept for the Scarran conference room.

Crichton

"Sometimes things don't happen quite the way you imagine them."

INT. GONDOLA ON LAKE

BLACK, WHITE AND RED CRYSTALS drop in a heap, creating a little mound in the center of the Gondola.

Some of the pieces bounce off the gunwales, FALLING INTO THE WATER WITH TINY SPLASHES!

PUSH CLOSE on the PILE OF CRYSTALS until camera finds —

THE WEDDING RING, intact, buried in the remains.

SUPER: TO BE CONTINUED

THE END OF SEASON FOUR

"Each and every year, at the end of the season we have a chat with you, our slightly bent cohorts in this wonderful adventure, and we wanted this year to be no different," David Kemper announced online on the evening of Friday 6 September 2002. "However, despite our best efforts, this year is a bit different from all the rest. In the past twenty-four hours, I have been inundated with emails and calls regarding rumours that are circulating regarding our joint passion.

"Where do we stand? We are two days away from shooting the last scenes of season four. As you know, SCI FI has picked us up for fourth and fifth seasons. However, as with everything done at a corporate level, there was an out clause built into SCI FI's pickup schedule. As of yesterday, we were informed — after massive efforts by everyone at Henson and working on the show, most importantly Brian Henson and the three gentlemen here — that SCI FI was not going to exercise its option to pick up the fifth season of *Farscape*.

"The rumours that everyone has been calling me about are sadly, very sadly, true. Tuesday will be the last time Ben dons the uniform of Commander John Crichton. We are all hugely sad. I am shaking as I write this. Yesterday, we all cried on the set. Yet, as we are, at the end of the line so to speak, being just the people who make the show, and not the corporate entities that fund and air it, we are as helpless as anyone. And we are sad. And we are shattered. And we are sorry. And we wanted to come online and talk to *you*, our core fans who have stood beside us for such a long and great journey.

"We all believed as late as thirty-six hours ago, that we were going to fifth season. But SCI FI has not picked us up, so, as all the rumours have suggested, we have no way to make the show. Believe me, Brian and everyone involved have gone *literally* to the ends of the Earth to make this happen, but there does not seem to be a way around this moat placed before us."

The news came as a shock to fans around the world, although the producers had been aware for some time that there was a question mark over the fifth season. The opening episodes of the fourth year had been specifically designed to entice a new audience to watch the show, but unfortunately new viewers hadn't even given the series a chance. The slipping ratings as the fourth season progressed were the final nail in the coffin.

"It was a very frustrating process," Brian Henson recalls. "We had set up a two season pick up, and it was very fragile. The show has always been right on the edge of possible. The SCI FI channel in America had a pretty small audience, so they were always spending the very most that they possibly could. The international distribution advances were always at the top end that anybody could justify, and seasons four and five were done as a package. Everyone knew it was a very tough proposition to put together. Everyone was right at the limit of their financing capacity.

"SCI FI changed all of their series orders down to thirteen episodes. They had budgetary constraints, and they tried to reduce *Farscape* season five from twenty-two to thirteen episodes. But that put an extra bit of strain on our other financing partners — and nobody could figure out how to get around it. It was the final straw that broke it all apart. If season

five had been ordered at twenty-two episodes, which was the original plan, it would have been OK.

"I was juggling balls between a lot of different people," Henson continues, "Hallmark, SCI FI and The Jim Henson Company. One group would have something that they needed, and we could just about make it work with the other two, then somebody else would change their position. Ultimately, it was a combination of SCI FI wanting to reduce their number of episodes, and the international distributors — the Jim Henson Company out of Germany — not being able to make their international distribution numbers work on thirteen episodes. It was very close. For about two weeks I thought I wasn't going to be able to put it together, then for two weeks, I was *sure* I was. It was about six weeks of hell for everybody. It's not nice to finish shooting a series thinking that you're going to come back for more, but it can also be very hard finishing shooting a series knowing that you're done! The way it worked out, our main cast knew for the last day and a half of shooting that the show was done."

Scapers immediately tried to rally public support, and, incredibly, managed to get the various parties back to the negotiating table. For one week, the sets were safe from the bulldozers. But in the end, a deal could not be made. Although some sets, and many of the vital props, were put into storage, *Farscape* shut down.

The fans didn't give up. They gathered together to create the Save *Farscape* Campaign. They generated petitions, and made it onto CNN. They created their own television advertising campaign. They held rallies in New York and Hollywood — with Ben Browder making an impromptu appearance when he saw the banners in Los Angeles on Halloween night. The cast and producers were amazed by the response: they had always known their fans were loyal, but this was simply beyond belief! The aim was to generate high enough ratings — maybe a 1.8 or even a 2 — to make SCI FI realise the error they had made. Maybe then they might reconsider.

"We never wanted to cancel it," SCI FI's President Bonnie Hammer

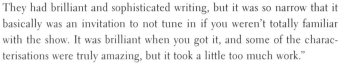

told *TV Guide* Online just before the final eleven episodes began airing in January. "What we were trying to do was do thirteen more episodes, not twenty-two. The ratings had softened, and it was getting increasingly expensive to produce. We just couldn't make the financial deal. But we never wanted it to end when it ended. We had all intentions of doing thirteen more episodes — we wanted to keep it in '03 and end it in '03. But financially, it was just too difficult to do.

"We love the series... and would have liked nothing more than for it to have had a little bit more of a broad appeal. If all of those incredible fans who wrote in and sent notes and flowers had actually watched it every week, we would have been able to do the twenty-two."

In Hammer's opinion, "*Farscape* got very, very serialised. It got very 'in'. They had brilliant and sophisticated writing, but it was so narrow that it basically was an invitation to not tune in if you weren't totally familiar with the show. It was brilliant when you got it, and some of the characterisations were truly amazing, but it took a little too much work."

Sadly, it seemed the fans' efforts were to no avail. When 'Kansas' aired on 10 January 2003, it got a 1.3 rating, and the following week 'Terra Firma' slipped to a 1.0. But the fans *still* didn't give up. An anonymous group purchased the front cover of the entertainment industry bible *Variety* to advertise the series at the start of February, and there was always the hope that another network might see the show's potential. Although the cast and crew would love to give the fans the fifth year that should have begun filming in January 2003, it became increasingly clear that this was very unlikely.

But the story is not over. Brian Henson believes that a straight-to-video anime adventure "as a test piece with potential for a series, is very possible", and that once *Farscape* is in syndication to a wider audience, "there's more of a chance of raising the finance and making a movie."

One thing is certain. *Farscape* brought people together from both sides of the camera, creating a global family who needs to know one thing — *what happens next?* ■

ell, we made it. All of us. To the last pages of the last book about the last season of *Farscape*. Don't know 'bout you, but that old axiom about it not being the destination that counts, but the *journey* itself, sure holds true for me. It was fun to watch, and fun to be a part of. What began so many years ago, as a disparate group of multinational individuals, grew inexorably over time into a family. And in that, I include you, the reader/viewer.

This 'family' business is my truthful, consistent, and final answer to the oft-asked question of, "What made *Farscape* so good?" It was common cause beyond the normal workplace mindset. We were closer than that down here in Sydney. What we did seemed to *matter* in a way I've never experienced in my twenty-four years of working in television.

Each and every person brought something of themselves; some little piece of magic no one else could have ever thought of. And in almost otherworldly fashion, these far-flung ideas somehow meshed. That was the other great strength of ours. We were a creative melting pot. Even more, we actively encouraged and *pursued* the unique, the surprising, the twisted. The shock was that everyone bent and shaped themselves to accommodate each new addition. Like a composite metal, this made us stronger than any one element on its own.

And, you, kind reader, were part of that process. You surrendered your preconceived notions about what a "space" science fiction show should be, allowing *Farscape* to ooze its way into your consciousness and in many cases, your souls.

Couples have met and married as a result of encounters in *Farscape* chat rooms and at conventions. Pets, and even children, have been named after characters in the series. An unprecedented, massive ad campaign was launched with *your* money to help save the show. Wow. You're as freaky for this thing as we are. And all of us on this side of the TV screen thank you for it.

So, this seems like a good time to ask, what happened to this fantastic thing of ours? Really? Well, politics mostly. Dollars, too. The people who bought *Farscape* (Rod Perth) and further developed it (Stephen Chao) were not at our patron SCI FI Channel when we were cancelled. Bad karma, that; but it's also the TV business. New people want new things, and they want to develop it themselves.

And, so, after all the explanations and protestations, we come to this, the final *Farscape* Companion. Sadly, as you may have already read within, no one felt or acted like we were at the end of our creative life. We were still smokin', as they say. And, "Yes", to answer another oft-asked query, we *were* deep into plotting our apocryphal fifth season, which stood, in my mind, to be our best yet. That's actually the biggest personal regret I have; that we didn't finish off the story. That our most fantastical, inspired and heretical moves remain unseen by the people we designed them for. As bad as you feel about it, Gladys, I feel worse. Maybe someday...

But enough wallowing. Forward. For all of us. We can either lament that *Farscape* is gone, or rejoice in the fortune to have had it in the first place. And, for that, some final expressions of gratitude are called for.

Thank you, Brian Henson, for deciding to do something that broke the mould, that challenged viewers and staff alike, and that would compromise nothing, most notably quality.

Thank you, Rockne S. O'Bannon, for the fruits of your incredible imagination. Thank you for the characters, the world, and the opportunity. Thank you for fighting when no one else believed. (And thank you for the marvellous word, *"Frell,"* which *will*, through ongoing popular usage, enter the dictionary someday!)

Thank you, Lily Taylor, for holding the show together. You are the unsung hero of *Farscape*. Thank you, Ricky Manning, for the brain that never fluttered; and for the clear eye through which *Farscape*'s insanity became focused. Thank you, Justin Monjo, for *being Farscape*'s insanity. And that's a supreme compliment.

Above: Executive producer David Kemper.

Thank you, Rowan Woods, Tony Tilse, Ian Watson and Peter Andrikidis, for your enthusiasm, creativity, talent and genius that gave Frankensteinian reality to black words on white paper.

Thank you, Claudia, Anthony, Virginia, Gigi, Lani, Jonathan, Wayne, Paul, Tammy, Raelee, Melissa, David, Rebecca and Fran, for marvellously interpreting the characters that *are Farscape*. Your inspired acting lifted us to undreamed heights. No one else could have played your roles. And, dear Lord, thank you *all* for being comedians.

Thank you, Dave Elsey, for the wonderfully warped vision that manifested itself in latex and foam. Your team of creature makers continued to astound everyone associated with the show right up until the last day. Grinning genius.

Thank you, Andrew Prowse, for the best friendship and collaboration I have ever known on a show. And for making the series you thought it should be. Lucky for us all it turned out to be *Farscape*.

Thank you, Ricky Eyres, Terry Ryan, Leslie Vanderwalt, Tim Ferrier, Russell Bacon, Guy Gross, David White, Deb Peart, and all the creative madmen and women at Garner MacLennan and Animal Logic. The combined outrageous, inspired, ingenious and original contributions of yourselves and your departments created the aura that we breathed like oxygen continuously for over four years.

Thank you, to *all* the people who worked so hard on the series, passed through *Farscape*'s orbit, or simply made a casual contribution. Each and every one counted.

And, lastly, thank you, Ben. First day, last day... Sometimes you get lucky. Sometimes it just works. *You* made it work. You meet the strangest people in the hallway out by the bathroom, bro.

If you're a *Farscape* fan (which is clearly a big "Duh, David" since you're still here at the end of Paul's wonderful fourth book on the subject), then these thank yous are from you, also — not just a final bit of self-indulgence on my part.

As you may have guessed, the family's gone diaspora by now, literally scattered to the four corners of the Earth. Everyone's on to their next thing, making films, TV, theatre, or just searching out peace and growth. But — and here's the good part — like any strong family, we'll stream toward home if the call goes out.

I have never written anything for the show, or to you, the fans, that I didn't believe in my heart to be true. Well, I do not honestly believe *Farscape* is over. I believe time and economics and the efforts of our extended family of viewers and critics will prevail. I believe I will work with all of my friends again in Sydney. I believe it will be on *Farscape*. Someday...

I really do.

And, lastly, allow me, on behalf of all of us, to thank *you* for watching the show and reading these books. I'd bet we'll meet again.

David Kemper
Sydney, Australia
February 2003

ust for now. The Last Word *for now*. Let's make that point exceedingly clear. Four seasons? The chronicles of John Crichton's remarkable journey have only just begun. Eighty-eight stories? The surface has barely been scratched.

And what of Aeryn, D'Argo, Chiana, Rygel, Moya, Pilot, Scorpius...? Their quests, their passions, their dreams can't scatter to stardust merely because we don't happen to be in touch at the moment. Like close friends with whom we've temporarily lost contact, they aren't gone, just living adventures we haven't been told yet.

And, knowing this crowd, they are some *frelling* great adventures.

Crichton and Aeryn left shattered in ten thousand pieces? *Hezmana* — they've gotten out of far worse predicaments than that! And what of Aeryn's pregnancy — surely any progeny of John Crichton and Aeryn Sun

Below: Back to the beginning. The crew of Moya in the première episode.

Next page: Series creator Rockne S. O'Bannon.

isn't going to let a little thing like a dimwitted business decision on a far distant blue marble of a planet blink him/her out of ever existing. A child from such a gene pool has got to be a willful little spitfire — determined to be born, to flourish — to ultimately mature to have adventures of his/her own.

Isn't that the way life works? *Real* life?

Farscape — not real life? When it's cooking, *Farscape* is complex and shocking and frustrating and hilarious and affirming. Isn't that *life* firing on all cylinders?

Even as you read this, John Crichton is out there... Aeryn with him... and all the others. (Crais! What of Crais? — surely he isn't gone for good. Any more than Zhaan is. Of that, I've always been certain. And Braca! I know we haven't begun to discover the depths of *this* guy!)

We need only stay diligent and keep watching the stars. And one future night there will come a familiar flash, an undulating blue tunnel will appear, and Moya will come racing into our lives once again.

I can only imagine the awesome stories our friends will have to tell us then...

Rockne S. O'Bannon
Los Angeles
February 2003

TO BE CONTINUED...

"That's not the language you need to learn," Chiana tells Aeryn in 'Unrealized Reality', but if you're stuck in the Uncharted Territories, or even Tormented Space, here's a few more words and phrases to help you get by...

Arky-Arky — Hynerian slang meaning smart-arse: Don't play arky-arky with me

Armarack — an amber-like substance used by the Tarkan Freedom Fighters to encase their precious stolen goods for storage in lava filled pools.

Arnooks — Nebari slang for breasts

Brontium — a pressurised gas used by the Grudeks in their Leviathan dissecting tools

C'Ztan Tool — used by the Tarkan freedom fighters to encase objects in Armarack, an amber-like substance able to withstand the intense heat of the asteroid's lava pools. The C'Ztan tool is also used to release the objects

Fannik — Nebari slang for the female reproductive organs

Fenik — Scarran for bastard

Fyang Powder — one of Noranti's secret herbs and spices. Used to put one to sleep

Gnik — an alien term of affection for an unborn child. Much like 'sprog'

Hapooda — an alien insult that has no literal translation but is so insulting that if used, it's capable of starting a riot (if not outright war)

Ka-le-nal — ancient Pilot for 'God be with you'

Kehr Tarklo — Scarran for 'sit down'

Klemmpt — Nebari slang for crazy

Ko-nach — Scarran for 'identify yourself'

Krillian alloy ore — a metal ore found in Leviathans. If the right equipment is available, Krillian alloy can be reduced and purified into a fuel capable of powering Crichton's module.

Leech Hypo — an alien hypodermic needle incorporating a living animal and used mainly by the Lukythians

Piezor — Delvian slang for bitch

Pislot — Hynerian slang for useless or pathetic

Possil — a mild concoction to dull the senses. Rather like a good Scotch.

Quarlark — an alien animal particularly resilient to odour. Hence the phrase: A stench coming from you that could kill a Quarlark!'

Rajnot — Kalish slang for idiot

Sha-kano-sho — an oath of allegiance used by the Kalish resistance

Shakta — a Luxan word for an untrustworthy, duplicitous person

Skernac — a Peacekeeper Special Directorate code known only to a few. It is powerful enough to save Sikozu from certain execution when Scorpius whispers it to her

Toubray — the nutrient rich tissue found in the Neural Cluster of Leviathans. Many cultures consume it to enhance higher brain function

Ucuz — an extremely hot alien fruit, that looks much like an apple, found on many of the planets in the Tormented Space

Y'Tal Cavity — a Leviathan's very first neural cell, the Y'Tal Cavity is a particularly rich source of high quality Toubray tissue. Once the Y'Tal Cavity has been severed, the Leviathan's Pilot and all its functions will cease to operate

Zyntian Filter — a piece of equipment that's installed in Moya's primary sensory nerve conduit to filter out the intense stimuli generated in Tormented Space

HAVE YOU GOT THE COMPLETE SET?

Don't miss out! The previous three volumes in Titan's bestselling Illustrated Companion series are still available.

Available from all good bookshops, or order direct on

UK: 01536 764 646
US: 01144 1536 764 646

For news on our latest titles email us at titan-news@titanemail.com

**TITAN
BOOKS**

Farscape © and ™ The Jim Henson Company